D1030005

HUDSON'S BAY TRADER

LORD TWEEDSMUIR

LONDON
ROBERT HALE LIMITED

TORONTO
NELSON FOSTER & SCOTT/GENERAL

© *Lord Tweedsmuir 1951 and 1978*
First edition 1951
Reprinted 1952
Second edition 1978

ISBN 0 7091 2423 6

Robert Hale Limited
Clerkenwell House
Clerkenwell Green
London EC1R 0HT

Nelson Foster & Scott
a division of
General Publishing Co. Limited
30 Lesmill Road, Don Mills, Ontario, Canada

ISBN 0 919324 37 1

Printed in Great Britain by
Lowe & Brydone Printers Limited, Thetford, Norfolk
Bound by Weatherby Woolnough Limited, Northants

ACKNOWLEDGMENTS

My grateful thanks are due to the Hudson's Bay Company, in whose Service I worked during the period covered by this book, for their valuable help on the proofs and with the end-paper maps. Most of the illustrations in this book are from my own photographs. Those on pages 33 (the lower picture) and 35 (the upper picture) are by my friend Chesley Russell. The photographs of the polar bear and the rock ptarmigan on page 157 are by Professor V. C. Wynne-Edwards, Regius Professor of Natural History, University of Aberdeen. Although these two photographs were not taken during the time with which this book deals, they seem to me to be so perfect of their kind that I have not hesitated to take advantage of Professor Wynne-Edwards' kindness in allowing me to reproduce them.

The photographs on pages 110 and 112 were taken by my Eskimo companion Otoochie.

I am indebted to the editor of *The Field* for permission to use certain parts of an article of mine in the Preface.

TWEEDSMUIR

April 1951

CONTENTS

ILLUSTRATIONS

HUDSON'S BAY TRADER

The Author, Baffin Land, 1938-39

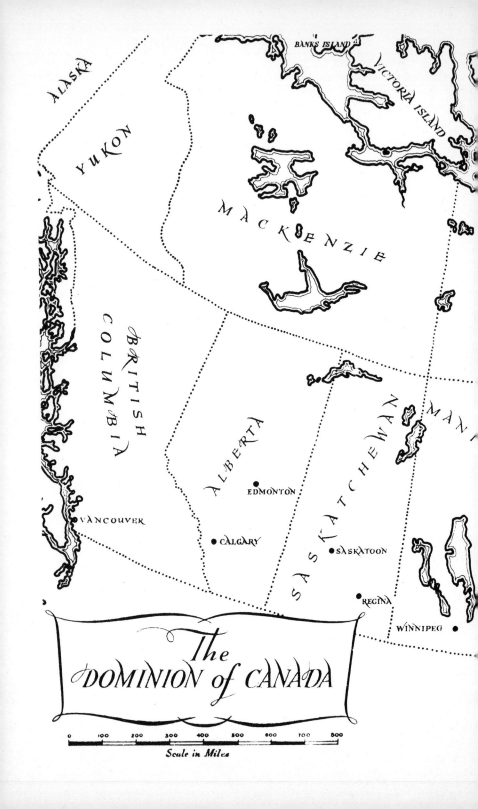

ALASKA

YUKON

BANKS ISLAND

VICTORIA ISLAND

M A C K E N Z I E

BRITISH COLUMBIA

ALBERTA

SASKATCHEWAN

MANI

EDMONTON

VANCOUVER

CALGARY

SASKATOON

REGINA

WINNIPEG

The
DOMINION of CANADA

0   100   200   300   400   500   600   700   800

Scale in Miles

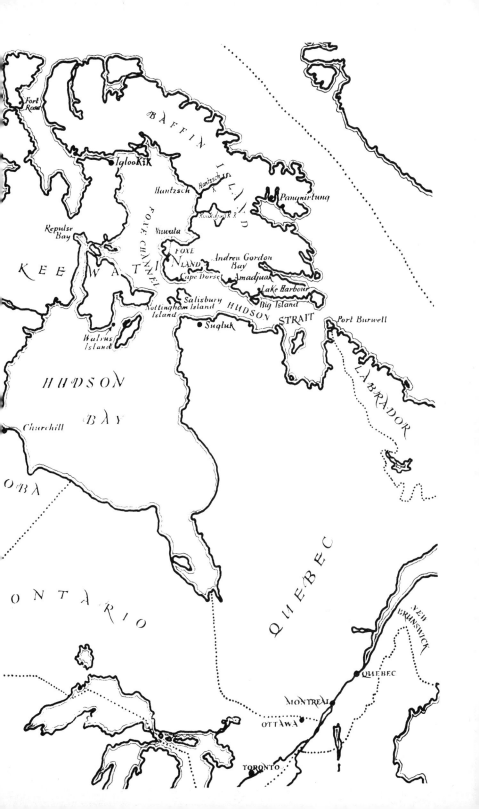

Fort
Ross

BAFFIN ISLAND

Igloolik

Hantzsch

Hantzsch R.

Panqnirtung

Koukdjuak R.

Repulse
Bay

Nuwata

FOXE CHANNEL

KEEWATIN

FOXE
LAND

Andrew Gordon
Bay

Cape Dorset

Amadjuak

Lake Harbour

Salisbury
Nottingham Island
Island

Big Island

HUDSON STRAIT

Walrus
Island

Suqluk

Port Burwell

LABRADOR

HUDSON

BAY

Churchill

B A

MAN

OBA

QUEBEC

ONTARIO

NEW
BRUNSWICK

QUEBEC

MONTREAL

OTTAWA

TORONTO

To The Governor and Company of
Adventurers of England trading into
Hudson Bay, and to one in parti-
cular of the Company's adventurers.
Chesley Russell.

PREFACE

THIS is a diary written with various stubs of pencil at latitude 64 degrees north. It has no pretensions to being prose. It was written in the course of a year spent in the Hudson's Bay Company's service at Cape Dorset. Cape Dorset Post is in Foxe Land, which is the south-western extremity of Baffin Land. Baffin Land is that vast, arctic island whose southern shore forms the northern side of Hudson Strait.

This diary was written at the Hudson's Bay Company Post by lamp-light in the winter, or by the never-ending daylight of the summer months, or somewhere between the two. But some of it was written in snow houses on the winter trail, lying in a sleeping-bag, comforted by the friendly roar of a Primus stove. Some was written by the pale radiance of a seal-oil lamp, in the snow houses of various Eskimos with whom I was lodging for the night. Some was written in a tiny wooden cabin in the bows of our little Peterhead schooner, which was dignified by the name of the fo'c's'le, where my eiderdown sleeping-bag shared the small surface of planking with the serpentine coils of the anchor chain.

The diary was written for something to do; and also from an unwillingness to allow so much that was so strange, so amusing, and so exciting, to go entirely unrecorded. Much of it was written with very cold hands. It was never written to be published.

In December 1939 I reached England with the 1st Canadian Division. My father, in Ottawa, came on the three grubby exercise books with the pencil scribblings. He had them typed out. The typescript has lain in a drawer ever since. By what lawyers call " The Doctrine of the Continuous Voyage " I suppose that I had always been headed for Arctic Canada. But it was a somewhat torturous journey. For I left Oxford in 1934, as a Cadet in the Colonial Administrative Service, bound for the Uganda Protectorate, with the intention of spending the

15

next 25 years of my life there. I fell seriously ill with amoebic dysentery, and was invalided out of Africa, and the Colonial Service, in under two years. I joined my family in Canada with an expectation of life limited to months. That winter found me far up in the forests of North Saskatchewan. The amoeba died game, but it was no match for 82 degrees of frost. No one knows the wonder of regaining health and strength, except those who have lost and found them again. That was in November 1936. The search for a profession combining adventure with some prospects, and a cold northerly climate, led me straight into the employ of the Hudson's Bay Company. Some months with them in London, was followed by half a year in Winnipeg and then I was posted to Cape Dorset.

The Company's small, sturdy Ice Breaker, R.M.S. *Nascopie*, lies now at the bottom of Hudson Strait. But then she was still serving the Company's northern posts, taking up goods and supplies and bringing back furs, in her one trip a year, when the water was open. Few ships could have been more beloved by those who knew her.

We sailed from Montreal on a boiling hot summer's day in June 1938. I was to meet my companion, Chesley Russell, at Cape Dorset, and replace his companion of the previous year, Herbert Figgures. Chesley, at 38, had had eighteen years' experience of the Company's far northern fur trade. He is still serving. He is a Newfoundlander, and his father was once skipper to Sir Wilfrid Grenfell. A better companion for a year of solitude no man could hope to find.

Herbert was a young Manitoba farmer, turned fur trader. He was to go to Lake Harbour, which was the next Company Post on that shore, some 350 miles distant. The Lake Harbour community were our nearest neighbours. Waiting, too, for the *Nascopie's* arrival at Cape Dorset, was my old friend Tom Manning. He was one of those Cambridge men who seem to spend the greater part of their time at Oxford. Even then, he was a noted Arctic traveller. Now he is famous.

In the *Nascopie* was the girl he was to marry. Every human

argument had been used to dissuade her from going to marry a man who lived in a tent or a snow house in the tundras. My own attempts at dissuasion went the way of the rest. We all agreed that no woman could possibly keep alive under those conditions.

Tom was waiting for her, when we arrived. His schooner, the *Polecat*, was at anchor, waiting to carry them up the western side of Baffin Land into the waters of the Foxe Basin, whose coast they were going to explore. They were married at Cape Dorset on board the *Nascopie*. The ring was a copper washer out of the engine room. I was best man. She survives happily, after several years in the Arctic in circumstances that would have finished most men. It is a very good thing to be proved completely and publicly wrong, every now and then.

Cape Dorset Post stands on a shelving, rocky slope overlooking a little cove. It stands in fact on an island. For the cove has a broad opening to the sea, to the East; and narrow rocky bar where the tides race, to the West. The Post is the conventional group of buildings that go to make up a Hudson's Bay Company Post. The trading store, and the fur loft above it, is the main building. It carries above the door, in the large lettering of a bygone age, the inscription

HUDSON'S BAY COMPANY
INCORPORATED 2ND MAY 1670

Apart, is the fuel store where the dog-feed is also kept, the cartridge magazine and the fur traders' dwelling-house; thus no outbreak of fire could destroy the furs and trading goods, the fuel and the dog-feed, the ammunition and the dwelling-house in one blow.

All these buildings were solid except the dwelling-house. Chesley and Herbert pulled this down before the boat arrived, and from the boarding built a comfortable structure for us to live in until we built a new one.

As there is no timber for many hundreds of miles the *Nascopie* had to bring all the planks, boards and wooden shingles needed to build the new one. They made a disorderly mountain on the rocky shore above high-tide marks; and the cases, barrels and sacks containing merchandise for a whole year's trading made another. The crew and the passengers helped us to get the house started. With foundations laid and the uprights to form a skeleton, the crew and the passengers packed up their tools, and we said our good-byes.

From the shore we watched the anchor come up and watched her turn slowly and then head for the straits. Her siren woke the echoes in the limpid Northern stillness of the Midnight Sun, and then we were looking at an empty harbour.

We had a house to build. We had trade goods to unpack, and sort, and store. We had the entire male Eskimo population to outfit for their Autumn hunting and their winter trapping.

The intervening ten years have perhaps brought many changes to that part of the world, particularly the demands of war and the strategic importance of the Canadian Arctic to-day. But, when I was there, few of the Eskimos had ever seen an aeroplane, or more than a handful of white men. Supplemented by the trade goods they got in exchange for their furs, their economy was based on the wild life of the land. If they are to continue to prosper it always must be so. The hunting of the walrus herds, and the harvesting of the fish that swarm up the river in myriads during the short summer, provide food for the sledge dogs for winter travelling. Walrus hide as well as seal-skin, cut in strips, takes the place of rope; and walrus tusks take the place of wood, whether for harpoon head or net-making needle. Sealskin is material for summer tents, and clothing, and the seal-oil lamp provides light and warmth for the snow house. The sadly reduced caribou herds furnish the warmest of all fur clothing, and deer sinew is the thread by which garments are sewn. The big square-flipper seal is the wrapping for the kayak. The skin of the polar bear is a warm carpet for the snow house floor. And all these beasts, and several others, are good food for the Eskimo. The snow is the making for his winter house, and he melts it when he wants water,

18

Thus equipped from nature around him the Eskimo can set about the acquisition of some worldly wealth.

The Company does not use coin of the realm in these remote parts. It has its own trade tokens with a fox's mask graven on them. The Eskimo starts with a clean sheet at the beginning of the trapping season. He receives an advance to the value of his proven skill as a hunter and trapper.

All winter he patrols his long line of fox-traps. The white fox goes across the counter of the trading post, and in exchange come the rifle and the ammunition, or powder, caps, and lead ingots, for those who still prefer to load their own cartridges. There are steel fox-traps, netting twine and needles, sacks of flour and sugar, packages of tea and coffee, square plugs of tobacco and cartons of matches. There are bales of duffle blanket and skeins of wool. As the trapping season goes on the shelves of the trading post empty, and the fur loft above fills with clusters of white fox furs, suspended from the rafters. There is other coinage besides the white fox—the rare and precious blue fox; the occasional white bearskin; the silver jar seal; the beautiful, but coarse, arctic wolf; and the tiny ermine weasel.

When the Eskimo is clear of his advance, he can lean his elbows on the counter and linger deliciously over his purchases, while the oil lamps flicker on the counter and breath rises like white steam in the cold.

Thus the Company has traditionally traded furs. Its form of trading must constitute the most highly-tested, and the smoothest-running, form of gentleman's agreement ever known in the world of commerce.

Thus, too, Chesley and I spent the 269th year of the Company together, We had no mail and we did not miss it. We had a wireless set that we very seldom used. When we did, we never seemed to get any news, which did not disturb us as we were not interested in the outside world. We got a weekly message from our families on this set when the reception was good. We had in addition a short-wave set with a morse key. We could get messages to Nottingham Island in the Straits where there was a wireless Post. They could relay to the outside world. Chesley got a good deal of fun from this instrument, and would talk shop to his friends in the other fur trade posts through the medium of the morse key.

In Britain we have probably carried the technique of sport to greater lengths of refinement than is to be found in any other country in the world. We fish not with the heaviest cast which the fish can be persuaded to overlook, but the lightest upon which we can possibly hope to hold him. We shoot birds not when they provide an easy mark, but if possible when they are at the pitch of their flight and only just inside the range of our weapon. Every possible point that can be afforded to the quarry is gladly conceded, because only then is success real achievement. When your livelihood and your very existence depend upon outwitting nature there is room for very few of these concessions. But that is offset by the fact that the quarry is seldom really easy. A companionship springs up between you and your weapon. Your rifle is your most trusty friend, who will never fail you, though you may often fail him. He stands between you and want, or worse, and is your constant companion, for in that remote country with its three seasons of autumn, winter and spring there is always something to hunt.

The autumn rains wash the last vestiges of snow from bare granite slopes. The arctic hare gets his winter coat of white, long before the new snow comes. You scan the grey ridges for the tell-tale white patch. More often you see none, until you start a hare from a rocky gully and follow him as best you can. He describes a great circle, squatting now and then to look round. You may miss him, but if you can keep him in sight you may get several more chances at him. At 100 yards his white woolly outline is a fair target. When the first snow comes he is easy to track but hard to hit, as he is only the faintest outline against the surrounding whiteness.

The hunting of the walrus is sheer necessity. You cannot but have sympathy for the hard-pressed herds or the great bolster-like figures lying on skerry or ice-pan, like gigantic editions of

Colonel Blimp. Rifle and harpoon, schooner and kayak are the means. The barbed ivory harpoon head is attached, by a length of sealskin line, to a sealskin blown up like a football. The harpoon head engages, the wooden and ivory shaft detaches and floats, and the great heavy carcass is held up by the floating football of sealskin. But a bull walrus, when roused, is an awkward antagonist. He weighs the best part of a ton, but he is a slow mover, for which I have often had cause to be grateful.

Characters stray in and out of the following pages but few need any formal description.

The Company's man at Lake Harbour was the vast, jovial Jimmy Bell, brother to one of the King's gamekeepers at Balmoral. There was a Royal Canadian Mounted Police Detachment, composed of Jock—who had been a shipyard worker on Clydeside—and Mac. You have to know a man intimately in Canada to know his surname as well.

In addition there was the missionary, Nielson. He was a hardy traveller with a dog team, and in respect to his cloth was always known as Mr. Nielson.

The Eskimo who appears most regularly is Otoochie. He worked for the Company at Cape Dorset and managed a team of dogs. No hardships and no difficulty could disturb his child-like and beaming serenity. It was impossible to be angry with him or even depressed in the company of this mortal. His name means, literally, " little seal basking on the ice." His wife, Wakta, made winter clothing for us, and stretched the white fox skins. She also did our laundry. But her temper was not so even.

Of the other characters old Saila was the patriarch of these scattered Eskimo communities. He had no formal position of chieftainship, as this is a conception foreign to these simple people. He was, nevertheless, regarded as a man who had seen much and knew much, and thus one to be listened to and obeyed.

Pitsulak was the paladin of his race. A skilful trapper and hunter, the best carver of walrus ivory on the coast, he was also an adept handler of a dog team, and a superb sailor. Unlike his brethren he was thrifty, and from his fur catch he had saved up and bought a schooner from the Company, as had one or two others.

Standing in the bows, with harpoon upraised in the walrus hunt, he looked like some strange Mongolian translation of the statue of the Discus Thrower. His name meant " the sea-pigeon." I always thought of him as that.

When we wanted an extra man for the winter trail or the schooner, we took Etidlooie. He was a small, grubby goblin possessed of great strength and a boundless good humour, untroubled by the possession of more than the basic minimum of intellect.

The only really unpleasant character was the medicine-man, Alariak. He was the only one who made me feel uncomfortable if my back was turned and he had a rifle.

There was a legion of others among this friendly race who contributed to making that year one of the happiest of my life. Twelve months can pass very quickly. When the *Nascopie* nosed her way inside the ice-pack a year later and dropped anchor, Chesley and I went out in our dinghy. People were leaning over the side looking at us. I did not know there were so many of the white race in the world. Our own world was so complete, and so absolutely contained by its surroundings, that I had come to think that Chesley and I and the people at Lake Harbour were the only ones.

That was in August 1939. The 269th year's trading of the Hudson's Bay Company was completed. Chesley and I went aboard, found ourselves learning, in a matter of minutes, of the awful momentum of European events during the past twelve months. Thus Munich, Czechoslovakia and the rest had passed unnoticed until the moment the *Nascopie* arrived.

The Hudson's Bay Company Trading Post as the author first saw it

The author's first sight of Chesley Russell

Chesley Russell laying the foundations of the traders' house at
Cape Dorset

The completed traders' house in which the author and Chesley
Russell lived at Cape Dorset

1

NORTHERN OUTPOST

July 24th–August 5th.

WE arrived at Cape Dorset on a calm, bright morning. Rocky mountains with rounded outlines reflected in a glassy sea. A few seals watched us, sank and rose again, their shiny heads leaving a faint line of wake as they swam. The inlet twists round, and ends in a *cul-de-sac* lying parallel to the coast of the straits. The familiar colours of the Post buildings showed up like a citadel among a scattered mass of Eskimo tents. All those Eskimos who had kayaks lifted them into the water and converged on the ship's gangway, scattering like birds before a hawk, to let the Post motor-boat through.

There followed a brief two days of hurrying backwards and forwards, unloading cargo, shaking hands with myriads of Eskimos, farewells, tots of rum and the old Hudson's Bay greeting, "A good winter to you."

Thus began the 269th year of the Company's trade in the North, and for me the first.

For twelve days Chesley Russell, Herbert Figgures and myself lived a life of eating heartily, sleeping and doing odd jobs. First the Eskimos who had come in for their trapping supplies from Nuwata and Amadjuak had to be packed off. There were days of counting out fox-traps and packets of cartridges and keeping your patience while their eyes strayed round the shelves wondering on what to expend their last few skins of credit. Then afternoons in the loft above the Post, writing up accounts. In the quiet dusk of the loft there were packing cases piled up, shelves full of sealskin boots, or piled high with walrus tusks, and hanging from nails in the rafters two bundles of white foxes, which had been brought in too late for the last fur shipment.

Finally, the house. It had been left by the ship's carpenters, a skeleton of uprights and roof beams, but luckily a complete skeleton. Day succeeded day, and when work was over every evening it looked slightly more like a house than it had done the evening before. There were variations. Tom Manning and his wife left in the *Polecat*, loaded heavily with a winter's supplies, bound west and then north for the Koukdjuak River. They sailed in dead calm and even-down rain, perched on the cargo, a perch they shared with three Eskimos and nine dogs.

One evening Herbert Figgures and I crossed the harbour in a canoe to look for a lost dog. We found his tracks in the sand by the water's edge. They led us along the beach and over the rocks and through a curious little glen full of thyme and moss into which our skin boots sank and squelched at every step. There was a moorland smell there and a little tinkling stream. We did not find the dog, but picked some flowers; we were then galvanized into tension by the sight of a black object in the water, and stalked it until it resolved itself into a bunch of seaweed, instead of a seal's head. As we undressed that night, we heard the dog howling across the harbour; we found out later that it had gone wild and was beyond our power to help.

August 5th–September 12th.

We breakfasted at a fire on a clear sunny morning which promised a warm day. The time had come for our trip to Lake Harbour with the dual purpose of taking Herbert Figgures to his new Post and 37 natives and 19 dogs on the first lap of their journey to Fort Ross. We used the schooner belonging to the Post. Chesley stayed behind. For two days we travelled under ideal conditions, dropping our anchor the second night out at our destination. A painted ship on a painted ocean, we chugged along.

Three times our water-breaker ran out and we stopped to replenish it. It was a slow business, collecting rain-water from cracks in the rocks, with an enamel tea-cup, and then pouring it in. Seals rose languidly to the surface; six Winchester carbines would crack like a badly synchronized machine-gun, and with a reproachful look the seal would submerge again. Figgures and I were behind two of the carbines, and Eskimos behind the four others. One seal, only, was hit, and he sank instantly, leaving an ugly smear of blood on the blue, glassy surface. The carbine costs the Eskimo several fox-skins. He would shoot straight if he bothered to clean it.

There was little room to move on board. Figgures and I cooked our meals on a primus stove; the food was thickly enriched by the hairs of the moulting dogs which blew into the cooking pots. You cannot blame a dog for what happens to his fur after it has parted company with him, but you can reproach an Eskimo for sneezing into your food. And we did. Dogs and men seemed to grow dirtier, more dishevelled and more depressed as we proceeded. The women were all down in the hold. They rocked their babies to sleep and cooked in front of them, with that bovine stoicism that centuries of getting the dirty end of the stick have bred in all primitive women. At times we were almost out of sight of land, and at times the bare rocky coast was above our heads. It would have passed for Ross-shire or the Faeroes at a casual glance.

Off Amadjuak we were among the islands, low rocky islets that looked as if no man had ever set foot on them. Certainly only a handful of white men can ever have landed on them. The natives had reported seeing white foxes there, but we saw none, and fewer eider duck than we had expected. How anything could support life there is a mystery. As it grew dark we travelled channels barely thirty feet wide with a foaming tide running through. It seemed as if we were drifting down a narrow greenish stream which flowed from nowhere to nowhere. It is the curious feeling of unreality which wild places give you that constitutes a great deal of their charm.

I slept through Figgures' watch and took over at 5 A.M. The sun rose over a dead calm ocean. At about seven we emerged into open sea. There were a few large bergs. They seemed to stand motionless in the vast blue mirror. One was shaped like the gable-end of a cathedral, another like the truncated feet of a crusader's statue. We began to hug the coast. Every turn of the helm seemed to produce a coast of different coloured granite. A more desolate sight can hardly be imagined than mile after mile of grassless, treeless granite. Even such birds as we saw, looked at us as much to as say, "Men don't belong here. Be careful."

At about 3 P.M. a strong breeze came up. I was sitting on a large packing case, just raising a rifle to my shoulder to salute a bunch of eider ducks, when something crashed behind me. Next moment I was held by one arm in Figgures' grip with my feet just clear of the water that hissed along the gunwale, amidst the shouting of men, the barking of dogs and the grind of shifting cargo. My few Eskimo words deserted me and I bawled feebly to the stern to "let go the main sheet." The boat righted herself, the Eskimos righted themselves, I crawled into position. The mast had not gone. All that had happened was that the steersman had changed the tack and let the boom swing across at breakneck pace nearly overturning us.

After that our course was serene. We travelled the length of the Big Island, then Lower Savage Island, the evening sun gilding the granite, and turned into Lake Harbour fiord. There was a camp of Eskimos there; they stood silently along the cliffs watching us, silhouetted against the pale evening sky. Three hours later we sat down to a cup of tea in the Post at Lake Harbour, whiskered, tanned, hungry, happy and above all sleepy.

I stayed two days, with the Jovial Jimmy Bell. Two days spent in eating far too much. I said good-bye to Figgures and the Eskimos. We wished each other luck. I left these hospitable quarters on Tuesday, the 9th. Weighed anchor at 1.40 P.M. The weather was dull and cold. Then rain came on, and with it a strong wind. We made good time down the straits with the sails set and a strong tide. The wind dropped and the rain grew heavier. We fired sporadic volleys at the seals that drifted up to look at us.

As night came, a thick fog rolled up with a heavy swell. Next day we rocked along in a leaden sea, chilled to the marrow. The coast that we had seen in bright sunlight three days earlier looked austere and forbidding.

We nosed our way into Amadjuak Bay in the evening. The Post there has been abandoned for some years, as being uneconomic, but as we landed it looked as when it was built. There was some coal left there, and we wanted it. The place was curiously forbidding. In the dwelling-house everything was as it had been left, crockery on the shelves, saucepans hanging on the wall, books in the bookcase. I reserved a bed for my own use, a soap-dish, a file, and a copy of *The Three Musketeers*.

Then came the work of loading the coal which was the real object of our mission. We waited until nearly full tide and then beached the boat. We had to break the lock of the coal-shed door, as it had rusted away. We packed 8,000 lbs. of coal down a hundred yards of sloping shingle beach and into the boat; myself and four Eskimos. By the time we had finished, it was pitch dark and we were dog-tired. With an Eskimo I returned to the house, and with the help of a torch, unscrewed the bookcase. It was eerie work. I shone the torch on the worn, mildewed volumes. The first one that I saw was *The Setons*, by my aunt Anna Buchan (O. Douglas). We locked up the house and got on board. The boat was high and dry and at an angle of 45 degrees or so. We filled the kettle full of eider ducks' eggs, boiled them hard, and ate them. Then we slept.

We set out next morning on the way back to the Post with grey mist drifting and a suspicion of a gleam on the ripples. Then thick fog came down. Our visibility was often only fifty yards. We threaded the narrow channels between the islands in a thick fog blanket. It was dead calm, with a chill in the air. We kept a look-out in the bows and, time and time again, wheeled the boat as the ghostly green of a limestone rock surged up from below to meet us. Or again we would hear a gentle lapping and a moment later there would be a reef before us, grey water lapping gently along its hog's back. But when

29

we anchored for the night the fog rolled back and the stars came out clear and frosty above us. Next day, at midday, we sighted Cape Dorset stretching out into a calm and chilly sea. That afternoon, washed, shaved and in clean clothes, I sat down to a meal of fried eggs washed down by one of the remaining bottles of Chesley's stout. It was August 12th, and a lot of grouse in Scotland would be dead already.

2

WALRUS HUNT

August 13th–31st.

WE worked away at the house and saw it slowly take shape. Windows and doors went into place, then partitions and more doors. Finally it was completed except for the long and tedious job of painting. We moved the stove in, and our beds, and spent our first night there. Then once ensconced we let the rest go hang and concentrated on the things that had been left undone. Our coal that was lying out in the rain was put in the coal store; and all the stores heaped up in there were removed and put in their proper places. The books were attended to, packing-cases opened and the contents put on the shelves that we hope will be empty when next the ship calls.

On August 30th the police boat from Lake Harbour came in and dropped anchor. We had been expecting her. Jock was on her bound for Salisbury Island to hunt walrus. He came up in the *Nascopie* with me. A Scotsman from Greenock, who having followed almost every calling under the sun, joined the Royal Canadian Mounted Police. He stayed all the next day and we prepared for the hunt.

September 1st.

At 9 A.M. we set out from the Bay. Jock's police boat went in front. Pitsulak's boat, the *Agpa*, towed us and we towed the *Mietik* which had no engine, only sail. Outside the Bay a thick mist hung over an oily swell from the west. Slowly we chugged along tumbling in the swell. I tried to read, then sleep, was finally sick over the side and felt much better. In time the tall crags of Salisbury Island loomed over us, and the fog dispersed. We chugged along slowly and opened one narrow ravine after another along the cliff, not a hundred yards distant. We saw a solitary walrus. It was getting dark, and we were anxious to get to our destination, so we left him. At 8.30 we opened a large bay and, guided by the light of a lantern waved by Jock, we dropped anchor beside him. There were five boatloads of Eskimos from Sugluk as well. Sugluk is a Company Post on the south side of the Straits.

It was a clear frosty night, and I went over in the dinghy for a cup of coffee and a chat with Jock. When I came up on deck my boat had drifted. I managed to attract two Eskimos, who had not gone to sleep. They are almost impossible to rouse when asleep.

September 2nd.

I woke up next morning early to the sound of the anchor being raised. As the coils of anchor chain were by my feet the noise would have roused the dead. We all set out for Walrus Rock, about ten miles distant; it is a tiny, low, rocky islet which at certain times and seasons is covered with walrus. We found none. The police boat which had gone on ahead did find one in the open sea and killed it. We returned to anchorage and were left from 11.30 A.M. onwards with nothing to do.

At 5 P.M. I went ashore to replenish our water-breakers and collected strange Arctic flora, which grow in the shape of pin-cushions. Then Jock and I stretched our legs on a sandy beach. We saw three separate fox tracks. There was little life on this island. A few polar bears and one or two caribou, and the foxes. As we stepped into the dinghy we heard the noise of geese. We saw them high over the Bay in a perfect wedge, the slate colour of the blue geese relieved by the white of the lesser snow-geese. That was the third flock we had seen in the day. They were headed south. Their drifting clangour came down to us, as they turned their backs on the North.

That night I had a meal with Jock and afterwards lowered myself into my dinghy. It was a calm, starlit night with the

Eskimos at the Post to get their outfit for the hunting season

The author, very new to the North, photographed on arrival at Lake Harbour

Chesley Russell looking for seals

Eskimo traders at the Post

Old Saila with the author

Eskimo children, whose reward for facing the camera was a gift of sweets from the author

Otoochie's son, whose name means "There is an occasion for rejoicing"

Northern Lights striking upwards on the horizon. I paddled to my own boat and found an Eskimo sharing my cabin. It was rather nice to have some company.

September 3rd.

We set out at 5.30 this morning for the Rock. There was no wind but a heavy swell, and the air was milder. There were three walrus on the rock, two old ones and a young one. The shots from the police boat drove them into the water. They scattered and we chased them. When they rolled they showed a long expanse of brown, wrinkled backs, in which our bullets cut red slashes. Cruel work, but necessary if our dogs are to have their feed this winter. They were weakened by loss of blood and their dives became fewer and their pace slowed.

When they submerged we followed them in the boat. They showed as pale ghostly shapes under the water that was growing scarlet round them. Then one rose beside us. Two harpoons flew, with the sealskin line attached to the sealskin bladders on the end. One bladder caught for a moment round the mainstay, and swung the boat over on her side before it jerked loose. Pitsulak's boat secured the other. The youngster died mercifully with a bullet in his spine. Nothing left but to collect the bladders and cut up the walrus. It took half an hour to cut up the big one. When we had finished, a strong wind came up from the west. We battled against it, and, deciding that our anchorage was too exposed, went two miles farther up the inlet. There we stayed until dark. Two Eskimos slept in my cabin. They both had bad colds, and as we were packed like sardines I shall probably get it too.

The gear for walrus-hunting is worthy of mention. First, the ivory-headed harpoons with the detachable tip to which is attached the sealskin line. The line is attached by a loop to a shaft so that the two do not part company, when the head detaches. The line is about ten feet long and is attached to a wooden plug at one end of the bladder. The bladder is a sealskin blown up at the other end where there is an ivory ring fitted in and corked with a piece of wood, like the bung in a beer barrel. The skins still have the flippers on them which stick out when they are blown up and give the appearance of some strange animal, plump, mute and imploring.

September 4th.

Bright and strong N.W. wind. Far too rough for the hunt. At about 7 A.M. ten blue geese and one snow-goose pitched on the beach two hundred yards away. They stayed there for about half an hour then rose honking loudly and settled in formation with the snow-goose at the head of the V. The rocky shore of the inlet threw back their clamour to us. They seemed to say "We are going south and we care not who knows it." In the summer all the geese in North America come here to breed, as do eider ducks, wading birds and two kinds of falcon. The sun shone all day. I went ashore in the dinghy for a short time. There were boggy hollows full of plants, notably grasses and reeds, and a kind of bog-cotton. One instinctively looked for snipe. We killed time until evening. The Eskimos practised harpooning.

September 5th.

We approached Walrus Rock in a dead calm. The sun was just showing over the horizon. We sighted three separate herds of walrus ploughing along. We have chase, a boat to each herd. The Eskimos sent up weird catcalls of excitement. For two hours hard we killed ten and managed to tag eight of them. It was brutal work. There were three in particular that swam side by side. Every time they appeared they were slashed with lead. When they were tagged the old bull turned, roaring on the boat. His tusks ground along the planking but did not enter.

As we started to cut up, a very strong W.S.W. wind got up, rocking the boat so violently as to make footing on the deck extremely dangerous. I looked down into the cabin and saw that it was awash with blood which had come in under the bulkhead. We retired to the lee of Walrus Rock to cut up our last and largest walrus, and arrived home at 4.20 P.M.; the sun never deserted us, but it grew very chilly. By dark the police boat had not returned but two other boats were in. We transferred our catch to the *Mietik* as did Pitsulak his four.

September 6th.

Off at five this morning in the teeth of an east wind. No walrus anywhere. Returned to the anchorage and breakfasted on the police boat off fried walrus. Then we went ashore and explored. Guided by a curious screeching we pressed on and found three red-throated loons screaming happily on a tarn together. They did not object to us; they had probably never seen man before. We found a sheltered place in the rocks where we smoked and then, discovering that our dinghy was sixty yards from the water by the ebb-tide, struggled back with it.

Borrowed a piece of soap off Jock and washed my face and hands in a bucket of cold water. Slept and read all the afternoon in my cabin. It smelt, and still does, of stale food, Eskimos, fresh blood, with the addition of warm tin and methylated spirits when tea is being made. One of the Sugluk natives brought me a blue goose, but I had to refuse it as it was out of season.

Sharing a small space with two Eskimos is making me rather like an Eskimo myself. The other night I was struggling out of my sealskin pants. One Eskimo signalled to the other who immediately laid hold of them and pulled them off for me. He returned a courtly bow to my thanks, as of one gentleman accommodating another. Their politeness would put the French to shame.

September 7th

No hunt to-day. A raging west wind forced us to move our anchorage to the neck of the inlet between high bluffs. The sun shone, but the wind bit. I paid a visit to the police boat and had a glorious meal of fried ham and potatoes in their jackets. Jock and I spent a busy two hours writing down the Eskimo for English words conveyed by pantomime. The word "altogether" defeated us after fifteen minutes' vigorous mimicking.

Went ashore and collected some plants and watched the white horses running in the strait. Went to police boat to borrow a book, and while I was in the cabin the anchor dragged. I was emerging to get my dinghy when Mowra and his two trusties scrambled on deck, grim-looking as death, and dived for the engine room. Fifty yards to the lee was the bluff, dark and forbidding, to which we were drifting like a racehorse. Order was restored, and, returning to my ship, I read and smoked until dark.

September 8th.

Another day of inactivity. A gale lasting all day long from the N.W., with an overcast sky. Visited Jock and lunched with him, and went ashore in the afternoon just to feel the land. Bumped the dinghy rather hard on the beach getting off again.

The Sugluk Eskimos put out their kayaks and paid no attention to the rough water at all. No birds visited us except an occasional loon, calling overhead. Chesley was once three weeks here trying for a load of walrus; hope the same thing doesn't happen to me. Got a lot of reading done. Had supper with Jock and sang all the Scots ballads that we could remember; hit my head an awful crack while getting out of the dinghy.

September 9th.

Left at six this morning. Met a very heavy swell off the inlet. At Walrus Rock there was but one occupant. Carbines banged and cracked from the *Agpa*, and the sea that foamed up the rock had a crimson patch in it. They never found him. We turned back and moved N. up the coast. Round a headland we sighted three walrus. The mother was carrying the young one on her back, the father looked like a nice old general. We gave chase. Three times they came up to blow leaving a white tablecloth of foam, then Providence was kind to them; the wind veered to N.W. We lost them and battled on for another few miles until we reached a bay formed by three giant and stony mountains.

We got up the mainsail, turned her head and went for home. It was wildly exciting. We tore along pursued by great blue combers that hung over us, picked us up, to go brimming on up to the horizon. It was sunny with a snap in the air, like a fine December day at home. I understood for the first time why the Clippers used to set a screen behind the steersman, as the sight of a following sea is so intimidating. Got into our anchorage at 3.30 P.M. Jock has returned but not the Sugluk boats.

September 10th.

Left at the unconscionable hour of 3 A.M. Heavy swell with a strong N.W. wind. Water foaming and booming round Walrus Rock. Jock was there pursuing a herd of five. We chased three, lost them and joined pursuit with Jock. It is the etiquette of the walrus hunt that it is your walrus if it has your harpoon in it. We got all five walrus, but it was difficult and dangerous work. We beat Jock whose big boat couldn't manœuvre as easily as our own. He touched the rock on one occasion but didn't damage his boat. Then they found that the sea had stove in their canoe, which they were towing, and getting it aboard took all their time. We corralled the herd in the angle of the rock where a reef juts out, and got every one. Cutting up was a lengthy business with the heavy sea, but we were back in the inlet before midday

Jock and I went ashore and climbed up the rocks. A curious desert of rocky mountains, shallow lakes, and strange Arctic lichens and mosses in all the hollows. I found a skull which I laboriously carried back to the boat. It turned out to be a walrus.

Why it was there I don't know, walruses not being addicted to climbing high mountains.

Cut a fine piece of walrus steak and fried it for supper in the police boat. I came up to get my dinghy. It was a cold, still night. A small, faithful little figure rose up from the deck. It was little Etidlooie, who had waited there to take me home. He thinks that I shouldn't be trusted alone!

September 11th.

Another very early start, but conditions perfect. Dead, flat calm. The Rock was covered with walrus, and everything was ideal. We must all have got out of bed on the wrong side as the harpooners missed their aim time and time again, but we got nine, and Pitsulak six. I harpooned one as we went by. I flung my harpoon with all the force I could muster and drove the head five inches home in his back; a bullet in the neck ended his troubles. We now have thirty-five walrus, which is a great improvement. As we came back down the inlet a flock of fifteen blue geese and one lesser snow-goose passed overhead so low that I could have got an easy right and left.

Jock came over and I boiled some coffee in the kettle. I had just finished my mugful when I discovered that the mug I was using had been employed in bailing walrus blood out of the hold.

As I sat down to write this Diary I was told that there was a gathering of seals at hand. Up they came and I steadied my rifle on the mainsail boom. I under-estimated the range and kicked up the water just on this side of one. The Eskimos chortled.

Etidlooie has now gone to make me a cup of tea. He is a faithful little grubby goblin. Sitting down here in my cabin it is very chilly and there is the strong salt smell of blood everywhere, which is varied by an unpleasing smell of warm tin when the kettle is boiled. Loons fly high down the inlet. Their call is like a farmyard symphony in which the duck and rooster predominate. Finished re-reading *Dracula*.

September 12th.

Woke up to N.N.E. gale. Hunting out of the question, so stayed in my sleeping-bag. A big lot of geese came overhead and their clamour seemed to fill the inlet. Etoodluk came in yesterday and suggested that the *Mietik* should try sailing home. Tookeke was non-committal. Finally decided that it was too risky and told him to stay. I think Etidlooie wants them away so that provisions may go farther. Shared out all the ducks' eggs to-day, handed out tea, tobacco and matches. The biscuits are almost exhausted but we have enough tea for about three days, some tobacco and plenty of matches.

We require about five more walrus, big ones, to fill our own hold. The *Mietik* and the *Agpa* are quite full. The journey back is going to be very tricky, as we shall be towing the heavily loaded *Mietik* and be heavy ourselves.

The smell in my cabin is getting very strong as the walrus is beginning to get high. Etoodluk has just appeared with a ptarmigan that he has shot, but what is one ptarmigan among twelve people? Glass falling like a stone: wind rising to hurricane proportions; outlook in every way bad.

September 13th

No hunting again to-day. Wind abated considerably but gigantic sea running. There is a continuous thunder from the rollers against the peninsula that forms the seaward side of the inlet. Heavy rain all day. The smell of decaying walrus is becoming almost unendurable. Gave out the last of the tobacco. Spent almost all day in my sleeping-bag learning Eskimo words and dozing. Our position now is rather like one of those games in which you may get to the end of the board at top speed but you have to throw a double six to finish. Got the Eskimos to sing songs in the evening. Pitsulak is unwell and is leaving for Cape Dorset to-morrow morning.

September 14th.

Left about 6 A.M. in heavy rain to hunt. Thick fog and very heavy swell. The *Agpa* kept pace with us to the mouth of the inlet and then headed for Dorset. We blundered about in the fog for hours without ever locating Walrus Rock. Finally we came on Jock cutting up a big one. Then we came home. The first thing that we saw in the inlet was the *Agpa*. Heavy seas and engine failure had forced her back. They had shot a loon and were eating it. Dreadful day of icy chill and dripping fog. In the evening a strong wind of ½-gale force got up from the N.W. Very cold.

September 15th.

Left at 6.30 A.M. Half a gale from N.W. Jock wouldn't risk it and put back again. We went on. Sea got very heavy and we tore along with mainsail and jib. Thought that we were going over several times. Found one walrus at the Rock but he gave us the slip in the heavy sea. Turned round and came home. Sea got very big indeed. Arrived back at 9.40 A.M. A lot of seals in the mouth of the harbour. Wish we could get one to give us something to eat. In the afternoon a peregrine came over the inlet. There was an ivory gull on the water and she stooped three times at it, just to frighten it. I know that manœuvre so well and that gesture of raptorial boredom. Decided for a seal, later on, went down the inlet in a canoe with Jock and a native. Saw a string of seals and fired one shot, nearly deafening Jock. Missed, of course. Seals fired at from a bobbing canoe are pretty safe. Cold, and outlook in all respects poor.

September 16th.

Pitsulak left at 5 A.M. to run for Cape Dorset. We went out to the Rock. Fresh N.W. wind with biggish swell. Jock who got there ahead was hotly engaged with a school and had tagged

Three schooners, two of them owned by Eskimos, setting off for the walrus hunt

Looking for walrus off Salisbury Island, Hudson's Strait

A herd of walrus off the bows of the schooner

Harpooners on board the schooner during the walrus hunt. The harpoons are tipped with walrus tusks

Hauling a heavy walrus aboard

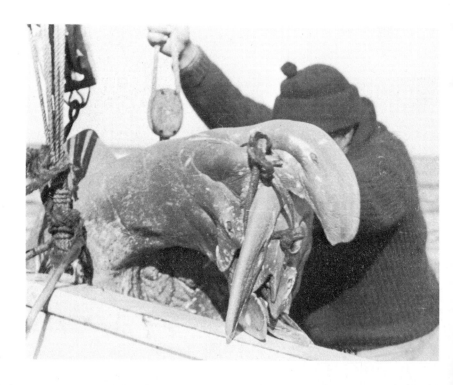

one already. We followed another school who were heading east. We opened fire at 250 yards with every rifle we had. We had to get them at all costs. Soon we saw the foam round them turning crimson and then we were among them. One old bull charged the boat to subside under a blistering fire at point blank range.

Cutting them up was difficult in the heavy swell and by the time we had finished we were some 17 miles from land. Engine behaved badly on way back. We have now forty walrus and are heavily loaded. We will set out for Dorset on the first fine day, towing the *Mietik* that is bigger and heavier than us. The glass is falling, curse it. One bright spot is that we have plenty of fresh walrus to eat. To-morrow we shall be out of tobacco. Pray Heaven it is calm.

September 17th.

Woke up to strong wind and bright sun. By noon it had dropped and we meditated a belated start for Dorset. Just then two figures appeared over the hill. They were Soloman and Ping-waktuk. Pitsulak had got no farther than the next inlet on the day before and he was now in need of petrol. We sent them off again hot foot to join P. telling them that we would meet up at sea and give it to him.

At 2.20 p.m. we hauled up our anchor and shouted good-bye to Jock, and, towing the *Mietik*, set out. Jock was going to make his load and then go back direct to Lake Harbour. The sun was shining and the wind had fallen. There was a fair swell at sea but we bumped along with our ponderous consort and our spirits rose. There was no sign of Pitsulak off the inlet, and we plugged on.

In the Bay of the Three Mountains we saw a school of walrus in the water, and, as we passed close in to the shore, we saw ten lying asleep on the shore. They looked like enormous slugs, ponderous and content. Just round that headland our engine petered out. We started to slip back towards the headland, rolling badly in the swell. We changed a plug and got going again. Then, as evening light died slowly away, the wind began to get up from the N.W. The light died and we began to pitch more and more in the gathering sea, and the jerks on the tow rope became more brutal.

At 8.20 the *Agpa* caught us up, she was pitching heavily too. We got our dinghy into the water and Etoodluk and Otoochie went across. They rocked ferociously in the rising sea, delivered the petrol and fought their way back. We hauled them on board and got the dinghy up and then started.

A most memorable night. We got the mainsail up and *Mietik* raised main and jib. We began to pitch and roll harder and harder. The waves looked hard and slippery to the touch as they hissed away to our lee, except where the breaking crests lit a thousand candles of phosphorus.

It grew black dark, a thick darkness through which the stars showed as pinpoints you could feel. Two noises added themselves to the turmoil, the hiss of flying spray and the flapping thunder of our mainsail. Putoguk held the tiller, his feet braced against the gunwale, Otoochie was at the mainsail, Etoodluk, down below, sat over his engine. Etidlooie and I stood by. Their faces, screwed up against the spray, exhibited only that quiet calm of fatalism.

I went below and braced myself in a corner of the engine room to get warm. Three times Etidlooie called down for the lantern. It lit up a small section of sloping, streaming deck and threw a light on the flapping, cracking sail. He was signalling. About a mile to the west a small spark answered us. It was Pitsulak, but each time there was a sickening moment of apprehension that there would be no answer. That spark lent us courage, a spark of human sympathy in that bedlam of tossing black water.

It was 12.10, when our engine gave a cough and petered out. The *Mietik* was on us in a bound. The steersman heard five cries as one, and just managed to get to our windward, but he was powerless to stop. A moment that seemed an age of clawing at the tow rope with numbed hands and we had it free, not a second too soon. Another moment and the rope would have come taut, and our stern would have been jerked round with only one possible result. Then we were alone and it was every man for himself.

Somehow or other Etoodluk got the engine restored and again we were scudding along. We flashed our lantern and far away to the lee we saw a tossing spark. It was Pitsulak, the "sea-pigeon". Of the *Mietik* there was no sign.

I went and lay down in the engine room. Etoodluk put a pillow under my head, and, soaking, I slept. I woke up at three, stiff and cramped. My head was on Otoochie's chest. He was worn out and slumbering. The sea had gone down a little and it was a little lighter. There was a thin crescent moon, across which the storm track tore, and the stars were brighter.

A ghostly shape surged up close to us. It was the *Agpa*. There was no mistaking that figure in the bow poised like the statue of the discus-thrower; it was the "sea-pigeon". In a moment it had gone. Etidlooie managed to make a cup of tea, holding kettle and stove down with one hand and holding on with the other. It was scalding hot and seared our throats. I wondered if there really were men who did not feel fear. I curled up again beside the engine and slept.

It was 5.30 and daylight when I awoke. And most wonderful of all sights, there was the coast of Cape Dorset solid and familiar, with the sea boiling round it. The mainsail was down and the jib up in its place. Ahead was the *Agpa* and two miles behind was the *Mietik* with all sails set. We were almost home. Reaction set in and we laughed and joked shakily.

Then Nemesis came on us. Without a second's warning, a screeching gale hit us from the west. With a crack like a gun, our jib halyard parted and we were on our knees retrieving it, with the wind tearing at us. The *Agpa* had turned and was headed back. As they sped past us the "sea-pigeon" raised his hand and pointed. We knew that the *Mietik* was in desperate straits with her spread of canvas, but if anyone could help her

51

it was that doughty seafarer. It took one hour to make a mile and a quarter and then we were in our own bay and the anchor down. Half an hour later Pitsulak joined us, towing the *Mietik* with him.

The walrus hunt was over. We were back, and not a moment too soon. The storm raged all day with a force that we could hardly have survived, and we were snug and comfortable, if a little bleary. How great a part Luck plays in all our fortunes. There aren't any cards in your own hand, above ten.

3

WINTER

A QUIET week of tidying up the Post and putting in walls, ceiling and floor in the porches. On Friday night the door opened to admit a dismal-looking object called Shooviga. He had come in to report that the fishing had failed completely up the coast, that the rock-traps had yielded nothing, and that he and his friends were relying solely on the good offices of Chesley and the Almighty to save them from starving. Their reliance on the former was not misplaced and they retired with some pockets of cartridges, some powder and primers for those who loaded their own, and some tobacco. Their thanks were profuse.

On Saturday we went hare-hunting. The hares are now snow-white, and as there is as yet no snow, more than conspicuous. They show up like a lighthouse against the dun-coloured rock. We went over to Porkituk in the dinghy with the outboard motor. We broke the pin as we started, which delayed us.

It was a dull, cold afternoon, when we reached the meat-cache at Porkituk. We were all wet with spray. Otoochie was with us. We laboriously quartered the rocks (I in tall rubber boots). Drew a blank there, and got into the boat again. We pulled out of the inlet, rounded a headland and ran down it until we saw two large hares sleeping on the hillsides. We grounded the boat with as little noise as possible. Chesley went for the near one, and Otoochie disappeared over the shoulder of the rocks after the other. I held the boat. Chesley got his hare and went out of sight after another. I waited a long time and smoked several cigarettes. A seal came and looked at me. I sent a shot singing over his head, but he disappeared in a flurry.

53

Otoochie returned carrying a hare, which he laid down in the boat with the air of one not wishing to boast. It was shot perfectly, in the back of the head, to prevent injuring the body. Then Chesley arrived stumbling among the rocks. He carried three hares and had worn a hole in one of his skin boots. We moved farther along the coast. Otoochie and I puffed and panted up a rocky hog's back. No hares, but a magnificent view of wild mountains with inlets eating deep into them. Vast ridges of rock; white limestone, red granite and other more sombre colours.

We circled and returned to the boat and set out for home. Two hundred yards from the beach two seals popped up close to the boat. We missed all of them, three shots. How we did, I don't know; our bullets seemed almost to comb their whiskers, but miss we did. Otoochie, the marksman, looked on in silent scorn.

We were almost in the Narrows, two miles from the Post, when we saw a hare sitting on a hillside. We steered for him and Chesley and I set off after him. We had misjudged his exact position and after panting and sweating over one ridge after another, we walked right on top of him. He stopped for a second on a ridge before disappearing from our view. I flicked up the 200-yard sight and knocked a spurt of rock dust up at his feet. But we got him later. We saw him far on from the top of the ridge and converged on him quietly, picking our way. It was Chesley's bullet that found him. That night, back at Dorset, we sat down to a huge meal and were soon in bed.

September 25th–October 2nd.

Woke up to snow on Sunday morning. All week snow came and went. It is not yet quite cold enough for it to lie, though one day it was cold enough to freeze the foreshore and make the edge of the sea viscous with ice. On Monday we woke up to a N.W. gale. Our smaller boat, the *Ivela*, sail and a small engine, was careering at her moorings, and dragging her anchor. We decided to beach her. Chesley and Otoochie set out for her in the dinghy. I waited on the shore with the rope and the rollers. They reached the *Ivela*, got aboard and secured the dinghy.

I looked up from coiling the rope. The dinghy was thirty yards to her leeward and headed for the rocks on the south end of the bay. I set off at top speed down the beach. It was a half-mile run. Going through a pool of tide-water filled both my sealskin boots. I panted, cursed and stumbled along. Six husky dogs gave chase. I stopped and cursed them away. They were too hungry to be trusted if I fell among the rocks. I had no real hope of being in time and was only continuing my John Gilpin progress for the look of the thing.

When I got to the point where the dinghy should have been pounding, I found that it had missed it and was careering down an inlet beyond. By a short cut I made the end of the inlet with five minutes to spare. The sea was very heavy and the beach rocky. The boat would soon batter to pieces. I waded in. Three waves hit me and drenched me and the fourth brought the stern of the dinghy into may hands. I made a spring at it, got half in, when my legs refused to function. I was soaked to the waist and the wind was icy. I managed to fall into the boat and got the oars into the rowlocks and a strain on them just in time. Rowing with two oars, overlapping at the handles by nearly two feet is no joke. In twenty minutes I made as many feet. It was no go. Contrived to edge the boat across the wind into a sheltered spot and then beached her. I then ran back to where I had come from. Chesley had the *Ivela* grounded. My boots were flapping round my ankles and spouting water. Went back and changed and we pulled the *Ivela* up in the afternoon. There were no men, so all the women, with babies on their backs, and the children pulled on the rope. We landed her a good two feet above high-tide mark.

All the rest of the week we worked away at the house. Saturday was calm and cold and bright. We set out in the afternoon to hunt hares. The weather started to blow up slowly as we left. We got to Porkituk rather wet and beached the boat with some difficulty. On the way we had stopped for two seals. They could not have been twenty yards from the boats, but we missed them; we were rocking so much. We padded across a rocky plateau, crossed two frozen tarns, beside one of which we saw signs that a bear had spent last winter there, and saw what we took to be a hare. After studying it through the glasses we decided by a vote of 2 to 1 that it was a stone.

We told Otoochie to go on overland to a point on the next inlet and we went back for the boat. We went well going out of the inlet, got very wet rounding the headland, and plugged down the long bay. We saw eider duck on the water, which we scattered with a rifle shot, then a school of white whales. Somehow or another we never succeeded in getting our guns off at them. Then they submerged for good.

We picked up Otoochie, who was standing on a granite promontory. We set off for Dorset and very soon the spray was flying over us. Then water on the plugs, and the engine stopped. Otoochie and I kept her head to wind while Chesley changed them. We got back at last, chilled and wet.

We were sitting down to our evening meal when we saw the *Agpa* enter the harbour. The other two boats followed, laden to the gunwale with walrus. The walrus hunters had returned. They brought us letters from Nottingham Island radio station. They had seventy-eight walrus. As darkness fell the wind rose and with it came snow.

October 3rd–9th.

Winter is coming early this year. The hills, which last week looked like gingerbread powdered with flour, are now white, flecked with the black points of protruding rocks. The usual weather is a heavy, grey-white pall of mist that seems to hang motionless over the whole land. The water in the harbour is becoming viscous and "gluey" on the edge of the waves, but I still find it hard to believe that the sea really freezes all over.

This week has passed quickly in indoor activity, painting and bread-making. We have been painting the ceilings, an

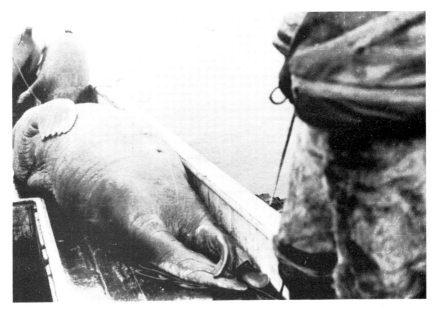

A small walrus on the deck

The schooner going through the ice-pans on the trip to Nottingham Island in the spring

The schooner hauled up by eighteen manpower

Chesley Russell with two Arctic hares

Chesley Russell with a very young Arctic hare in spring

Hauling the Post schooner ashore for the winter

arduous job carried on in a most unnatural position with the paint running down the handle of your brush and over your hands. Bread-making takes years off your life. It involves keeping the house red hot for a day and a night. The sleepless night ruins the next day for you, but it is worth it for the smell of the new bread alone. There is that sporting element of uncertainty as to whether or not the bread will rise, which gives a glow of achievement if it does. So far it always has.

Our Saturday hunt was a shining success. The pall of grey mist lifted and the sun shone. It was cold and crisp but the sun was bright and the weather was dead calm. It was too tempting to miss. We set out in the morning, and we had not gone a quarter of a mile before black heads began to pop up round us. Otoochie got one first shot. It looked small and pathetic as we dragged it aboard.

Otoochie sat in the bow with his feet sticking out over the gunwale. When a seal was in the offing he would scratch the gunwale with his finger-nails to attract them. Seals are naturally curious. Chesley was shooting rather wild. I was trying my ·22, but the cold had thickened the grease in the bolt and often as not the pin did not strike hard enough to explode the cap.

We re-started the engine and moved on. In the Narrows we met three of our Eskimos in a big canoe on the same errand. We gave them a tow; broke the rope; mended it and towed them until we saw the water dotted with black heads. We separated, and the Eskimos drifted away. We could see them standing up in a line, three rifles parallel, pointed at a target that was invisible to us. Then puffs of smoke and splashes from the bullets and the noise of the shots drifted slowly across to us. We sat in our boat and smoked and potted at the inquisitive seals that came too close. We got another five and gave up because there was no more room for them in the boat. As it was our legs were stuck in front of us, pillowed on their bodies. They were like small, grey bolsters, filling the bottom of the boat.

By then it was a beautiful day. The sun was warm on our cheeks and the sea without colour and without horizon. The

distant islands and shore-line seemed to float in space, their outlines obscured by mirage. The sun set a golden gleam on the
snowy hillsides.

We gave the entrails of our catch to the dogs. One tiny
puppy sturdily maintained his right to a share. How he managed
to avoid being crushed and bitten seemed miraculous. But
there he was on his wobbly, woolly legs in the heart of the tearing, snarling mob. He got enough to satisfy his small needs and
wobbled off again with his tiny tail curled over his back.

Chesley had shot a duck the day before so we were well
supplied with natural food. We dined off seal's liver. Eating seal
has an uplifting moral effect. You are satisfied to think that you
are living off the country, and you know that it is good for you.
When it also tastes good, as it does when well cooked, it has a
combination of qualities that few dishes can boast.

We had set up our receiving set in the afternoon. In the
evening we turned it on. It was like receiving a brutal blow in
the face. It let in on us in a flood that harsh and unlovely world
from which we had separated ourselves. A world of haste without speed, of recreation without rest, of feverish activity and
dissent, of cavilling and discord. We waited until midnight for
the Northern messages from station KDKA. It is in Pittsburgh
and sends messages to the North. Chesley received a message
but it blurred in the middle. But he got most of it and guessed
the rest.

Sunday was the usual pleasant routine of late breakfast.
There are few greater pleasures than sitting over breakfast, with
the knowledge of nothing to be done. In the afternoon we
practised with my ·22 on a rabbit face that I had cut of cardboard. We fired about twenty shots at it. It still maintained the
idiot expression, but we found that some of the bullets had
hit it.

Later I took my ·22 and wandered off over the hills. The
snow was hard on the little plateaus between the rocks, and
the heavy mist hung like fog. I flushed a hare and jumped as I
saw him. It seemed so surprising to see anything alive in this

curious silent desolation. He looked yellow against the snow, not like the hares of a fortnight ago who resembled gorgeous powder puffs against the dun-coloured rock, vaguely suggestive of pantomime figures. He bounced away out of sight. I followed his spoor, losing it often where the snow was hard and gave up as it started to get dark. By that time, I had done one and a half complete circles. I got back and had my Sunday shave by the lamplight. We had Chesley's excellent eider duck for dinner.

October 10th–15th.

All week we worked at painting the inside of the house. What we saw of the outside world was through windows misted over by the warmth of the stove. The slow rhythmic routine of painting makes the time fly faster than anything else I know, but it has a most unpleasant side. The fumes of paint got in our eyes and made them smart and run as if we were snow-blind. The evenings were the worst and we would suspend a conversation in the middle to mop streaming eyes. At times it would be so bad that we were forced outside into the darkness, to stand and shiver until our eyes were rested.

The *Keegarveealuk*, our schooner, came in on Wednesday from caching walrus. They had a quantity of seals. Pitsulak had ten to his own rifle. We got some written-off tinned food, set the cans in line and made them race from the store to them. Then we drew lots for the rest.

Chesley and I went on board the boat to take the numbers of their rifles. The same old smell of blood and grease, and damp, rusty rifles and oil. I have a great affection for that little boat, in spite of the smell.

No seal hunt on Saturday as we were too busy. The painting was over but we were staining the woodwork. Sunday was its usual peaceful self. Annie, our domestic help, fell asleep and so our luncheon was late. I did not start out on my hare-hunt until about 4.30 P.M. When I came back it was almost dark.

The snow crust was brittle and I made enough noise to scare all the hares in creation. It was good exercise. It was just sufficiently eerie alone in the frozen hills to give each expedition the flavour and fascination of an adventure.

Chesley had made a bookcase and set it up in the living-room. It holds all my books, neatly and exactly. It is a great relief to get them all under the same roof as myself. A bookless house is unendurable, even in Baffin Land.

It has been thawing and freezing alternately all the week. The snow comes and goes. But it will soon be winter in earnest. We shall both be glad when it is. The real highlight of the week was a dinner of muktuk, the skin of the white whale; it looks like silvery rubber, but is really congealed kid glove. We cut it in slices and boiled it. It was good in its way but very like eating goloshes. When not used as food, it is used for making bootlaces.

October 16th–23rd.

The weather has got much colder of late. There is a leather scum of ice on the edge of the tides. On Tuesday we went to look for our lead-dog, Kutchinaki. He had strayed from the Post, which means that he had done one of two things. Either he had gone to the caches of walrus meat at Porkituk or else he had gone to Etoodluk's camp at the Fish River. Of course, we chose the wrong alternative. There was no sign of him at the cache. There was no sign of fox tracks either which was depressing. Only a tracery of crow tracks and crumbs of dried walrus flesh sprinkled on the snow. At one side of the cache, a stone had come away and the head and tusks of a walrus looked out, for all the world like an angry old general. We shot a seal on our way home, or rather Otoochie shot it.

It was not till Saturday that we found time to follow the second alternative. It was very cold and calm. We crossed two shallow bars with the water running like a rapid over them and not a yard of water below us. We saw Etoodluk hunting seals and left him to it, chugged down a fiord with tall steep sides

and ground below the camp. Kutchinaki was there. He was tied to a rock with a long line culminating in a trap and chain fastened to his collar. He had the air of a schoolboy who has climbed a tree to steal apples and has had to summon the owner's help to come down again. Two women were making a tent; they seemed oblivious of the cold. We shook hands with an old woman with a tattooed face, bundled Kutchinaki into the boat, and set off home. I made him lie on my feet to keep them warm.

The only other outing we got was an afternoon stroll on Wednesday to clear our heads after bread-making. The snow was a fascinating carpet of tracks. No fox, alas, but hares by the score, a ptarmigan, and what was really remarkable, a day-old bear track. We saw none of the makers of the tracks but one hare. I knocked up a puff of snow just beyond him as he ran. I was pleasantly conscious of having made a good shot; to have hit him would merely have been a fluke. We needed that walk; the temperature in the kitchen was 114°.

My Sunday hare-hunt was a fiasco. The wind was blowing a full gale, carrying the snow along the ground, hissing like a boiling pot of white sauce. I had to battle my way back step by step and got my beard and moustache full of ice. I spent the rest of the time making pictures. The pictures are photographs cut from magazines, mounted on cardboard with electric tape and a window-pane; luckily we have a large supply of spare window-panes, tape and magazines.

October 24th–29th.

A very strenuous week indeed. We opened packing-cases, swept, tidied and succeeded in putting the store, shack and oil-store completely to rights. We walked up to the Lake one afternoon to see about ice for our winter water supply. It was frozen to the bottom and will be hard to saw. The usual practice is to saw big blocks and heap them up on the shore. When we want water we go up with the sledge and fetch a block. It was one of those quiet afternoons with the sky a hard, pale, orange. We saw no tracks at all.

The next afternoon we spent at the bar trying for a seal. The day was quiet and mild, with light snow drifting down. We scraped the snow off a rock and sat down. Chesley regaled me with anecdotes of his boyhood in Newfoundland. On the way back we saw a hare's track, but no fox tracks which is disturbing.

I sorted out all the books on Wednesday. I threw away five of them: three manuals on how to become a strong man in several lessons, an annual for girls, and a book on how to run a successful Sunday School. They landed flapping on the water, like half-grown mallard. I felt rather as if I had hit below the belt, they looked so pathetic.

We hunted seals on Friday, a really cold day. We visited the caches at Porkituk. No sign of foxes, not even a crow's track. On the hill above I saw an old type rock-trap for foxes. We had hardly got into the fiord again when we saw a seal. Chesley hit it very neatly but we did not get it. I missed one very close on the way home. We got back covered with frost. Chesley had a sore throat as a result of wearing no hood.

My Sunday hare-hunt was extremely strenuous. I started a hare bounding down a gully and pursued him for miles. The footing was so tricky that I could not take my eyes off the ground, so that I probably started him several times without knowing it. I followed his track until dark, and jogged home. This is the first week that I have had a radio message. One from my Mother over Station KDKA, Pittsburgh. We got some frozen fish from the natives; Arctic char and brook trout.

October 30th–November 6th.

The week started cold, very cold indeed. The harbour was frozen over completely on Monday. Chesley went hare-hunting and started my hare of the day before in the same gully. It followed the same track again. He did not get it and returned leaving a trail across the snow of two sets of hare's footprints and two sets of human ones. But no one would ever see it to wonder at it.

Tuesday saw the harbour still frozen, and five seals lying like fat old gentlemen on the edge of the open water, near the bar. The next day Otoochie, whose hand is against the whole animal creation, shot one of them. There was a seal, and if possible it should be obliterated, half a mile of thin ice notwithstanding.

We took an inventory of all our stock. Bags of flour, boxes of cartridges, canisters of powder, lead for bullets, rifles, traps, flour bags, twine, and a myriad other things. Otoochie finished the sledge; it is over twenty feet long, two heavy planks as runners, with boards across.

On Thursday some natives came in from Nuwata with sealskins to trade. They said that Tom Manning had been delayed there for six days by ice. We got a short-wave radio message from Pangnirtung saying that native caribou hunters had seen his boat at the mouth of the Koakdjuak. There was an easterly gale blowing all day, and it shifted most of the ice out of the harbour.

On Friday we woke up to find that the radio aerial had blown down. We rigged it up again, and in the afternoon were off hunting. We went right across the island without seeing even a track. There were great green seas rolling in from the straits and we watched them crashing and thundering against the granite. It is a sight one never tires of. We set a match-box on a stone and took shots at it. Chesley wiped my eye, but I retrieved my reputation somewhat by hitting it, edge on, in the snow after he had knocked it off the rock.

My Sunday hunt was longer than usual. I went to the south where the big mountain lies and a long way up it. There was a hard crust over soft snow and the ice tinkled at every footstep. The wind took the fragments and whirled them along the icy surface, making a noise like tinkling glass. I saw a fox track. He had been catching lemmings, and here and there there were red dots of blood on the snow. I dug down with my mitt but there was nothing else there. That was all the leavings of his meal. There were many lemmings tracks, pathetic little tracks, such as might have been left in *The Wind in the Willows*. But we shall trap that fox and close his account, and one day ours will be closed too, and so it goes on. The Northern Messenger, the official radio programme of messages to the North, started on Friday and I got a message from outside. Time is slipping by terribly quickly.

What a life this is! Peace, complete and perfect. No neighbours except the animal creation; a quiet routine of meals and varied jobs, sometimes hardship and risk, to add variety, and always that glorious cold, white silence.

November 7th–13th.

Winter has come in earnest now. For the first time we have had sub-zero temperatures. The harbour has really frozen over and the wind has piled and jumbled the ice round the edges. The temperature has dropped fast and ice gathers quickly on my beard.

On Saturday we went over to the bar to set a few traps. This gave me my first experience of cutting snow with our long knives. The trap is settled in an indentation in the snow. Then you cut out a block of snow, pare it into a round flat slice, and lay it on top.

It was bitterly cold and we had to wait for an hour to cross the bar. We stuck our knives and rifles in the snow and did cabman's flap to warm ourselves. The rocks on the bar were neatly encased in white. They looked eatable. We slipped and stumbled across, set two more traps and came home. We had a wonderful stew of hares and ptarmigan. The ice on the harbour shows pale lime-juice green in the afternoon light. That is the hardest colour in nature—the colour of submerged rocks, the colour of a green mamba.

A bright, cold day in winter. The photograph shows all the buildings that go to make up a fur-trading Post

Eskimos in the early dusk of a winter's day. First from the left is Pitsulak, then a famous hunter and trapper, now a legendary carver

Eskimo hunters on their trap line

Huskies beside a snow house. On the top of it is their walrus hide harness, out of their way

A fine specimen of the real husky dog

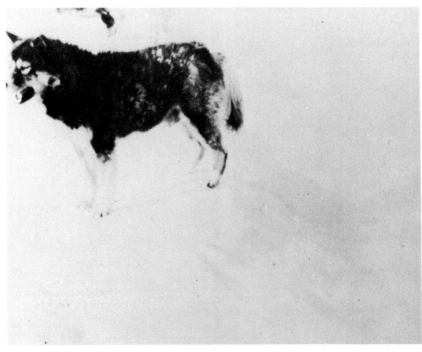

4

ALONG THE TRAPLINE

November 14th–20th.

OUR real trapping routine has started. Every morning when it is fully light we set out on our trapline. For three days we were setting traps and since then have been visiting them. The bleak fact stands out that we have not caught one single fox. Monday was a long day. We crossed the harbour, climbed the hills on the other side and put down eight traps. It was cold but we got very warm.

There were tracks of hare and fox everywhere. We set one trap beside a curious horny object, which stuck out of the snow. It was a whale's ear drum, so Chesley said. From that same place we could see in the distance Etoodluk's camp. It looks like a collection of tiny, smooth, white beehives.

Trying to cross the harbour ice on the way back we had trouble with the rising tide. We hopped from one moving, sinking ice-pack on to another, until we reached the main pack. It was no weather for getting wet.

On Wednesday we took the small sledge and went over to Porkituk. There are few things so intriguing as travelling on a sledge. There is so much variety. Speeding across smooth ice with the runners making a low rhythmic grumble, helping the dogs up a hillside, hanging on for dear life going down hill—legs thrust out one side, head and shoulders the other swaying and balancing—hauling, shoving and cursing the sledge through shore ice which looks like a giant's rock garden carved in greenish white chunks.

The dogs have each an independent trace all joining to the bridle, a ten-foot strip that goes to the sledge itself. In rough ice the traces get hooked on to projecting pieces of ice, and, his companions straining forward, the unfortunate dog is hauled backwards. There is a wild moment of uncertainty when you leave the dogs, and set out on foot to negotiate shore ice. As they break free, you must keep clear enough to avoid the out-lyers of the fan, and then rush in and leap sideways on the sledge as it hurtles by. It is rather like musical chairs, but with rather more at stake. The dog-whip is thirty feet long and made of seal-hide. The driver lets the lash trail behind the sledge and holds the handle in his hand. When cracked it sounds like a gunshot, and can cut through a two-inch board.

We took the dogs over to Porkituk and set traps round the cache of walrus meat. Otoochie helped me set mine, with the same kindly air of co-operation with which a keeper in England or Scotland shows the young master how to handle his first gun.

On Thursday a tremendous wind broke up most of the harbour ice but we went round our nearby traps. Saturday was a chapter of accidents. I ploughed through soft snow to my first trap, slipped and fell on rock, damaging my rifle and plugging the barrel with grit. Snow had drifted over my next two. The fourth had been robbed by two ingenious weasels. I rebuilt the set and the first thing I did was to slip on an icy sloping snow-bank and partially stun myself. I arrived back in a bad temper. My gun was none the worse except for a few scratches.

The ice has made again in the harbour. We spent a leisurely Sunday, visited some nearby traps, found that a dog had sprung one.

November 21st–27th.

Monday we went over to Porkituk with dogs. The going was heavy and our pace slow. The dogs as usual were frantic in the rough shore ice. One of them snapped his trace round a project-ing piece of ice and ran along dragging it. It was a mild day and we got very warm struggling and slipping in the rough ice, and undoing traces that had caught round projecting angles. Some-times we were not in time and the dog in question would be

74

hauled back, gasping, and pulled clear round the obstruction like a rope round a capstan.

On Tuesday we set out round our land-line of traps. Not a fox and not a sign of one. There were ptarmigan's footprints and hare's too, but not a fox.

We had difficulty in crossing the ice coming back. Getting on to the floe was successful but getting off we had to hop from one piece of sinking, moving ice to another. They were shaped like lily pads and the water hissed at the edges as we jumped. Where it showed beside the bar, the water was green *crème de menthe*. When I said this to Chesley, who had spent 18 years in the North, he asked what *crème de menthe* was.

Wednesday saw Chesley busy in the house. Otoochie and I took the dogs over to Porkituk, or rather they took us. Exhilarated by a snap in the air and the knowledge that they had only two instead of three passengers, they went like demons. In the rough ice they raced and plunged, while we clung to the sledge for dear life, over the piled-up slabs with the sledge crashing down on the far side, only to be picked up and whirled on like a leaf in the wind. It was very exciting. There were no foxes in the traps.

On the way back I hopped off the sledge to free a trace and one leg went through the ice. It was a chilly ride home after that. Coming through ice on the beach we were both flung off the sledge, and we saw the sledge careering onwards leaping high in the air until the dogs fouled the tent ropes of Otoochie's tent. This got their traces tangled and they started to fight.

Friday, my birthday, was beautiful, still and bright. The sun, hanging low above the horizon, threw long blue shadows along the snow. There was not a breath of wind. I crossed the harbour ice and slowly climbed the hill on the other side. The sunlight gilded the snow on the distant ranges. There were two inches of soft snow, and fresh hare tracks were deep. In one place there were ptarmigan tracks; the birds had sunk in deep, and their tails had brushed the snow as they walked. There was an Arctic hare in one of the traps; tracks led up to the others but their marks had stopped short. Almost all the traps needed re-setting. I sat down, smoothing the hard snow, covering the plate of the trap until it was paper thin.

Trapping is one of the most restful pursuits to the mind that I know. Your subconscious mind mechanically shows you the trail and is alert for tracks and any sign of life. Your real mind is hard at work confuting legions of opponents in some long dead argument, or preparing unanswerable ones for future use; thinking how silly you were on some occasion, and how clever on another. And all the time your feet are going thump, thump, thump in the drifts on the snow and crunching on the hard crust.

Coming back I had difficulty in crossing the shore ice. I had to use my rifle butt as a staff.   As I hopped and plodded across the ice-pans I must have resembled an ancient Hindu pilgrim on the shore of the Ganges.

On the next day Otoochie and I had a furious "John Gilpin" ride of two miles across rough ice. I fell off twice and thought we would break our necks. On our way back we found that two white foxes had crossed our track while we were away.

That evening Pitsulak arrived and told us that Tom Manning's Eskimo, Santayanna, had arrived at his camp; twenty-six days from the Hantzsch River. There were letters from Tom and some deer meat. Santayanna had told Pitsulak a rather remarkable story. The night before he reached Pitsulak's camp he was uncertain of his whereabouts. In his sleep he dreamed that half a mile from where he slept was a pile of stones, and a piece of driftwood stuck in it. He dug down and found ten hares. He took five for himself, and five for Tom.

Next day he went out to investigate on foot. There, as in his dream, were the pole and the stones covering a cache of walrus meat, and beside it Pitsulak's camp.

November 28th–December 4th.

Monday and Tuesday were spent by Chesley in preparing to go inland. On Wednesday we crawled out of bed at 5 o'clock of a chilly morning, had breakfast and set out in the darkness. We had a terrible time in the rough ice on the beach. On the far side of the Bay it was ten times worse. Low tide had left a wall of ice, and we slipped and swore and scrambled. Then the bridle broke and away went the dogs leaving us with an overturned sledge. It was Otoochie who caught them, fifty yards farther on, where they had stopped to fight. We got them hitched up again and ashore.

Light came slowly and drearily. The stars disappeared and the outline of the clouds began to emerge. The colour of the snow turned white instead of grey. By the time I left Chesley it was quite light. We had some coffee out of the thermos. I watched them carry on down hill, flounder in the rough slabs, saw Chesley thrown off the sledge on to his back, and far and faintly heard a flow of salty Newfoundland oaths.

I pottered off round to the traps. For once I had no rifle, for I couldn't risk carrying it loose on the sledge in those conditions. As luck would have it, I saw a ptarmigan. He was sitting on a rock above me on a slope, so confident of his protective colour that he never moved. He did not know that from where I stood he was perfectly framed against a dun grey background where the wind had whipped the snow from the lee side of a boulder. He watched me over his shoulder as I walked, both of us thinking that we had scored off the other. There was nothing in the traps, but most of them had been drifted over with snow.

The next two days I watched my short trapline. I caught an ermine which eventually may find its way into a peer's robe. On Friday night I made my début with the short-wave, morse code radio. There were two messages for Dorset. I tapped and faltered and dithered and finally got into contact with Nottingham Island. One was from my Mother. Alastair, my brother, had got something. Twice I had to tap back and ask what? I thought of all the things he might have got; a disease, a prize, a house, a decoration. Third time I was lucky—it was a bull-terrier!

On Sunday I did not wake till ten. It was a day so perfect that it made me wonder why everyone did not live in the Arctic. I wandered round my short trapline. I got to the headland and looked out over the coastline stretching eastward, and stood and drank it in. Running out from the shore was the floe bathed in purple shadow. Beyond that was the water with the thin ice in a pattern of different greens, like Waterford glass. The sun touched the coastline and turned the slopes of snow to an orange gold.

On it all was the stillness and utter immobility of everything that you see only in the winter North. It was so perfect, I felt no bitterness because my traps were empty and the cunning little ermine weasels had stolen the bait. I looked at the dainty tracks that the white fox makes, with his neat little paws, and felt friendly towards them. It is just these compensations in a country which is all hard knocks and buffets, that draws you to it.

December 5th–11th.

On Monday I ploughed round the long trapline. The going was bad and I did not get back until it was almost dark, at 2.30 P.M. Annie was standing looking out over the Bay thinking that I must have had an accident. I flushed five ptarmigan on that walk. They were soon whirling white specks far out on the tundra, and my eyes were blurred trying to follow them.

Chesley arrived at lunch-time on Tuesday. He had travelled hard since three that morning and was very hungry. The rest of the week went by as usual with Eskimos bringing in foxes. We asked one of them, Ashoona, what he thought of our new house. "I don't think about it," he said.

On Friday I caught my first fox. Poor little creature, I was sorry for him, but his troubles were soon over. Coming back past the place where I had seen the ptarmigan I found the same covey in the same place. They were standing in the pits they had dug in the snow and were eating something. One of them jumped out of his pit and stood still looking at me. His fellows did the same. They showed up an opaque white, on a glittering background. The sights of my rifle must have become deranged on my walk, because I hit the snow full two feet this side of him, throwing a blanket of powdery snow over him. The covey flew off cackling. I saw them later on a hillside as they took wing once more. There were signs of others, their neat little pits dug in the snow down to the sorrel.

On Saturday I was nearing the Post after working my short trapline when a big white hare got up in front of me, was over the hill in a twinkling and circled back past me. He was perhaps three hundred yards away and travelling fast. My first bullet went over his back and he doubled his speed; I fired again, this time wide, and he went even faster still. I stood and laughed as he receded into the distance, seeming to rise and fall as he tore across the undulating snow. On the other side of the hill I found Otoochie's little boy with his father's long gun. He had been stalking the hare before I flushed it.

Sunday has been a day of packing up to take the inland trail to-morrow, with Otoochie.

5

THE INLAND TRAIL

December 12th–18th.

ON Monday a strong wind prevented our starting, but on Tuesday we got away just before nine. It was mild and we travelled hard all day to make up for our late start. It was dark when we reached an old snow house of Chesley's, which he had shared previously with three Eskimos. There were tea-leaves and the bones of a hare on the floor; a block of snow cut into a cribbage scorer, with two matches stuck in it, showed that they had been playing their favourite game.

We lit the Primus stoves. Otoochie took the tin of stew and cut off both ends with his snow-knife, then he cut it down the side and removed the tin altogether, leaving a smooth cylinder of frozen stew. He boiled up some snow and put it in the stew. It was very good; he then boiled some more snow and made coffee.

That done, we put down two large bearskins, with four winter deerskins on top and unrolled our sleeping-bags on the top of that. Otoochie produced a frame shaped like a goal-post, stuck both ends in the wall of the snow house, and we put our mitts and socks on the wires that formed a net across the frame. The Primus was put underneath and the process of thawing out began. He had another implement shaped like a long wooden dagger. This was a snow-beater, and Otoochie thumped himself with it to rid himself of the powdery snow that covered his clothes like diamond dust.

It is surprising how poorly you sleep in a snow house until you get used to it. At least four times in the night, and on succeeding nights, I would wake, light a match and look at my watch. A small snow house can be comfortable in its way. You are tired and you get relatively warm, but your breath rises in clammy clouds, and when you sleep it condenses like cold glue on your sleeping-bag.

We woke next morning and had a mugful of porridge, with butter and sugar, and then black coffee and a cigarette. Then we rolled up our bags, put out the Primus and cut a block out of the wall of the snow house. A cloud of cold air billowed in like smoke, from a square of chilly black darkness. We rolled up the skins and our bedding and crawled out into the blackness. It was bitterly cold. The dogs were just visible as dim shapes.

Otoochie opened the thermos and took a mouthful of hot water. He spat it in small streams on to a piece of bearskin which he held in his hand, and then ran it along the runners of the sledge. He worked quickly taking new mouthfuls of water until he had covered the runners with a skin of ice. I pulled the rolled-up harness traces from the top of the snow house, undid them and laid them out on the snow, in order with the leader's long trace in the middle. The end of each is threaded on to the bridle. By this time Otoochie has loaded up the sledge and it only remained to catch the dogs.

We travelled on all day. It was too cold for a mug-up. We passed Mount Pingukyuak on the left and slid down slowly to the great prairie of central Baffin Land. There was a thick mist. My beard was stiff as brushwood with the frost. My moustache had large lumps of ice pendant from it. Our boots and mitts were stiff. This is what is known down-country as "the nice dry cold you don't feel." At 3.15 P.M. we camped. Otoochie built a very small snow house; we just fitted in, and it was really quite snug.

The next day was the same; slogging across a flat, pitiless snowfield. I found a fox in one of my traps. In the evening we stopped beside a lake to look for a trap of Chesley's, but we could not find it. At last in desperation we loosed the dogs. That solved the problem. In an unbelievably short time Tudlik was howling to high Heaven with the trap on her paw. We built an igloo with a large rock sticking up in it. It was made by candlelight.

Husky dogs resting on the overland trip. Each trace joins up to form a bridle which is tethered to the sledge

A brief halt on the inland trail

Husky dog team on soft going, with the whip-lash trailing behind

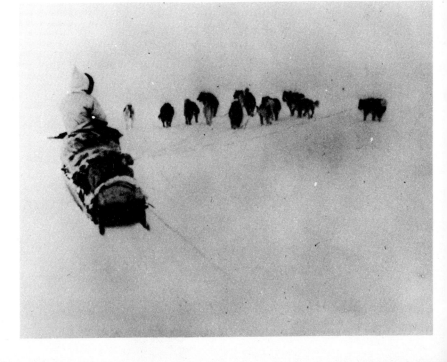

The author with some of a catch of white foxes

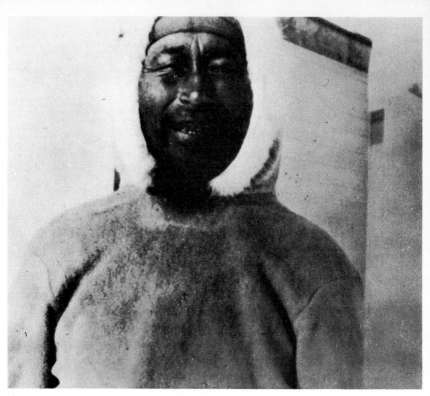

Shorti, the lay catechist from Lake Harbour

The next day was so cold as to be agony. We reached an old snow house of Chesley's and turned back for home; we caught one fox and one Arctic hare. The cold made our boots feel like wood, and I partially froze several toes. We camped in our snow house of the second night. The Waldorf-Astoria could have been no more welcome. We ended up by generating such a heat that the roof began to drip.

The next day we pushed on till dark and slept in the hills again. We passed two of Chesley's snow houses and had a long and tedious pull up the escarpment by Pingukyuak.

The next day travelling hard and fast we made the Post in time for luncheon. The going was good and we had a break-neck ride. Going down hills we had to lunge and lift the bow of the sledge to miss the rocks. Where it was very steep we put a band of walrus hide on one runner as a brake.

6

TWENTY-SEVEN BELOW

December 19th–31st.

A LOT has happened in thirteen days. We spent a quiet week
until Christmas Eve. We opened our presents which consisted of a book each from Bishop Fleming (Bishop of the
Arctic), and a parcel containing three bottles—whisky, port and
sherry—from Ralph Parsons, the Fur Trade Commissioner.
We drank all the port on Christmas Eve, while we listened to
the spoken messages from C.B.C. I heard my Mother and Father
very clearly, also Jack Fraser and Rupert Reece. It was a pleasant
evening. We tumbled into bed late, and tumbled out again very
late next morning.

We spent a peaceful Christmas Day indoors. Otoochie and
his family all had presents, and so did Annie. Annie gave us a
present too; a piece of soap. There was no hidden meaning
behind it! There was a high wind on Boxing Day, and Chesley
could set out.

On the following night Nottingham Island announced that
they had a message for me from Pat Baird at Repulse Bay. It
stated briefly that Reynold Bray was drowned near Igloolik in
September. I could scarcely believe it. I had thought that
nothing could have killed that shrewd little gnome. We tapped
all messages to and from Repulse Bay for three days, including
one from Tom Harrison in England. We got the details. Reynold
had been blown out to sea in a folding-boat, alone. Baird had
got a whale-boat out as soon as he could, but there was no
trace. It will be a terrible blow to Tom Manning. It seems only
yesterday that he and Reynold invaded my rooms at B.N.C.
the day that schools ended and, catching the general spirit of
hilarity, threw all my food and furniture out of the window.
Now his death made me terribly lonely. It was a storm in

Hudson Strait that claimed my greatest university friend, Christopher D'Aeth, in the same month, seven years ago. They were close friends those two. Chesley has been doing his best to cheer me up, kind fellow that he is.

On Friday afternoon Annie took offence for some obscure reason, as Eskimos do, and ran away after lunch. We thought that she had gone to camp. It began to blow up cold in the evening, half a blizzard in fact.

Next morning Etoodluk came in. He brought Annie; she was half frozen. His dogs had smelt her. She had gone out to sulk and had been caught in the blizzard. They warmed her up in Otoochie's tent and she was none the worse, though two hours more on the tundra would have killed her. Strange creatures, Eskimos!

And so ended the old year.

January 1st–15th.

This has been a quiet fortnight indeed. Chesley was away inland from the 3rd to the 8th. It was bitterly cold in there but he got eight foxes and ten hares, which made up for it to some extent. I spent a surprisingly busy time at the Post.

I am surveying the position of the Company's buildings, and my only weapon is the mariner's compass that a Peeblesshire neighbour, Jimmy Munro, gave me to take to Africa. I say nothing against this excellent instrument but it does not point to the North. Having no measuring chain, or anything like one, I measured off fourteen feet on my dog-whip lash and used that. It was a cold job but I finished it at last and plotted it on paper. Everything that could be wrong was wrong about it. I shall have to change my methods.

A good number of Eskimos came in to trade. Chesley made a bench for them to sit on, and we painted a draught-board on it. They played till nearly twelve o'clock each night, and I often played with them. Rules are no object to them and they would jump at any pieces from four whole squares away. It was great fun.

One night I was sitting up late and writing. I heard the frozen snow crunch by the window. I got up and went out; there, under the window, was a big box that we used for bringing in ice for our water supply. In it was an old husky dog. The box was half full of snow and he had curled up in it. He looked up at me appealingly, as if to say "Don't drive me away, please. I'm a poor dog, and my master's a poor man and I don't very often get a chance to sleep in a nice box, like this." I closed the door and left him. A husky dog's life is a very hard one.

It was on Sunday night that Chesley returned, late in the evening. We have fallen very much into a routine of eating, sleeping and trading. Our hours of daylight are short: at the shortest, evening begins at 2.30 P.M. When the light lengthens it does so quickly, and days are perceptibly lengthening. On Tuesday night we got a message from my Mother, mentioning the possibility of Pat Heathcoat-Amory flying up here. It will be wonderful if he does. He is a fearless devil and given ordinary good fortune could hope to do it if he tried.

The days are getting longer now. It isn't necessary to light the lamp until 3 P.M. That is a great relief, as life by lamplight is very tiresome. This week had been still and calm with the mercury low. My work of surveying the Post has been going forward slowly. Two bearings and a measurement, then a return indoors to thaw frozen fingers.

The mountains are magnificent now. Deep in shadow all day, their rounded summits are bathed in gold from the slanting sun, and the sky is a pale coral pink, with every cloud frigid and motionless.

One day succeeds another without obtruding on your notice. Life goes on, and every now and then you realize that days have passed, since you last thought about the calendar. The winter North has an astonishing beauty, and the mighty silence that hangs on the land seems a balm for all ills of the spirit.

Otoochie and his wife Wakta came in one evening to stretch

foxes. We played draughts together. Otoochie and I faced each other on the bench with the board between us. Wakta sat behind him, resting her cheek on his shoulder. She soon tired of the game and tried to hurry up her spouse who was deep in contemplation of each move. Finally she started to her feet. Otoochie tried to hold her back, but she chided him and, coming to my side, showed me a move that allowed me to wipe Otoochie out. Then, still chuckling, she led him off to his igloo.

January 16th–22nd.

Otoochie and I started on the inland trail at 7.15 A.M. It was 27 degrees below on the thermometer. We went first to Tesseyoumajuak and met Etoodluk there. He was not going inland himself but was sending his two henchmen, Pingwaurtok and Pudloo.

The sun came up as we pushed on, a crimson ball low down on the mountains. In the narrow valleys we were sheltered from the wind, and hauling the sledge through the soft snow made us quite warm. We caught up with the sledges in front; they were stopping frequently to look at traps. They had a fine team of dogs. Each dog had his name in Eskimo characters on his harness.

We took the lead of them. Darkness fell but we still kept going, and we crossed the mountains on to the plain. The stars were bright and there was a wisp of Aurora Borealis. One of our dogs, a small bitch, got loose and went straight into a trap. We heard her howls in the dark. The other sledge came up and helped us to free her. At last half frozen we came to an old igloo of Etoodluk's.

Pudloo and I went in and started the Primuses. The other two dealt with the dogs. It is the custom of the country that on such occasions the white man stands the treat. A can of beans and one of stew were hacked open and their frozen contents deposited in the cooking pot. We fed and smoked, the stoves were put out, and Otoochie and I climbed into our bags. The other two had no bags. They each laid down a dogskin.

When I woke up early next morning they were lying smoking, and suffering stoically. It was a bitter morning with a very strong wind. We plodded along. Our heads were caked with ice and there were frozen spots on our faces. At midday we came to another old igloo. We left the sledges and dived inside. All four of us were shaking with cold like four great dogs. We started the Primuses and thawed our hands. Our feet were numb and we still shook, but it was bliss. The three Eskimos took a large chunk of walrus meat and squatted round it hacking off bits and eating them. I ate half a pound of raisins.

When we came out again the dogs were curled like furry snails, backs to the wind, with the drifting snow piling up against them. We parted from the other sledge here. Darkness soon fell and we built a snow house. Few white men can build a snow house. It takes an Eskimo about half an hour. The blocks of snow are so solid, that it is like building with masonry. We were thankful to get inside as it was bitterly cold and still blowing hard. Nothing is more gorgeously clean than a new snow house. It is like a fairy grotto of an unearthly whiteness. The walls sparkle with a myriad diamond pinpoints. The next morning the heat of the occupants will have turned the walls into ice, opaque and lustreless. There will be tea-leaves and coffee-dregs on the floor, sooty stains from the candle on the walls, and a debris of match-sticks, cigarette and pieces of paper everywhere. The two wooden boxes and the stoves will have left their mould on the floor, but it has served its purpose.

What a strange substance is snow! At once your enemy and your means of life. The blizzard is your greatest enemy. Then the fall of heavy flakes—which obliterates tracks and wipes out visibility—which in the North they call "Snowing Hudson's Bay blankets", has brought many of the hardiest travellers to losing their way.

"He lost his way" needs no further explanation in the North. It means the end. And yet without snow you could not travel. You build your house of it, you eat it in your stew, you drink it in your tea, you ice your sledge runners with it. Its omni-presence detaches from the world as you know it and makes the North a world of itself.

The next day was Wednesday. It was even colder but there was less wind. The sun rose not as a ball of fire but as a pale gold orb with a pear-shaped aura round it of the same colour. At each side were two great rainbow sun-dogs. We examined a lot of traps and found not one fox. A ptarmigan had walked over the plate of one of the traps but had failed to spring it.

That night we camped in an old snow house of Chesley's at the end of the trapline. It had been left unblocked and the snow had drifted in. Inside it was piled up in the shape of a wave-crest. Otoochie went in with his saw, and cut it up in blocks which he pushed through the opening to me. Meanwhile a hungry dog had stalked up to the sledge and abstracted a frozen trout from a sack of trap bait. I chased him with the whip and he dropped it.

Otoochie sawed away until the floor of the igloo was flush with the outside snow. This meant that the roof was very low but the house grew beautifully warm. We heated it until it dripped on us.

I questioned him about the Toonit, the race of dwarfs that are supposed to inhabit central Baffin Land. I told him about the Picts and the Congo pygmies. I probably left with him the impression that England was filled with little naked men who used blow-pipes. I drew him a picture from memory of a Pictish dwelling in Shetland. He was very much intrigued.

We had a long talk sitting on the deerskins before the stove. Otoochie stirred his tea with a cake of snow and rolled one cigarette after another, as he told stories, occasionally laying a small brown hand on my own, and squeezing it, to drive home some point.

I am a very bad linguist, but it is possible to learn any language in the world if you are forced to it. Eskimo has 500 endings to a verb and nine cases to the noun. But the learning of this particular language is made easier for the

Otoochie on the coastal journey

Otoochie building a snow house on the Foxe Land trail. This photograph was taken in the spring at midnight

Otoochie giving the dogs a rest on the trail

Otoochie by his sledge in the coastal hills during the return
journey from Lake Harbour in the spring

Loading up the sledge after a night in an Eskimo encampment

foreigner in the Far North. Such is the natural politeness of the Eskimo that they use only those words which they think their visitors know.

Furthermore, when the visitor has blundered ungrammatically through a sentence, they tell him with a disarming smile just how he should have said it!

Having listened to Otoochie's stories we unrolled our bags and slept. One of the most annoying things about the cold is that it interferes with your night's sleep. Not that you aren't warm in the bag. You are, snug and comfortable, but your breath condenses on the bag in hard white frost, and as you roll over in the night you get a faceful of slimy ice.

Next morning was bitterly cold. The dogs plodded along in bad snow. Our faces were badly frost-bitten. At 2 P.M. we reached our snow house of the second night. We piled in and heated some coffee on the Primus. We got our hands warm but nothing else. When we came out again the dogs were all lying in the lee of the sledge. They looked at us as much as to say, "You might think of the comfort of us four-footed fellows."

When we found a snow house that evening Otoochie was so cold that he jumped off the sledge and held both his hands to his face. His nose was freezing. We thawed out gradually in the snow house. Otoochie produced the hare, our only catch, and hacked it in two with his snow-knife. The knife made a noise like an axe falling on wood. He sliced it up, peeled off the fur and boiled it. When he had finished it he picked up the cooking pot and drank off the juice, breaking off now and then to tell how good it was. He looked like a squirrel with a nut.

We were cold in the night and next morning was a bitter one. A strong wind with snow limited visibility to about 80 yards. Three times we nearly gave up but thought better of it. We were cold and weary and hungry when we nosed our way into an old snow house in the hills and knew that next day we would be at home.

The last day we pushed on through the mountains. There was a bitter wind and our faces were badly frost-bitten, when we finally descended to the ice. The dogs felt the sea-ice and revived. We sped along in the gathering darkness, the outlines of the land just visible with light snow coming down with the wind. Otoochie sang to the dogs and cajoled them. Every now and then he would put his arms round me and look into my face to see if it was frozen. Once he said my nose was frozen and, taking his warm little brown hand out of his mitt, held my nose until the blood came back to it. We didn't care, we were near home now. Soon the flag-pole was above us on the land, just discernible against the grey of the sky.

Twenty minutes later I was in the Post, Chesley was frying venison in a pan and I was slicing up a ham for a royal feast. I pulled off my clothes and as my hood came over my head it caught the bridge of my nose and pulled off the skin. But I didn't care. I was warm now.

7

WINTER SUNSHINE

January 23rd–February 5th.

THE sun has appeared again. The daylight is lengthening. Instead of a pink light slanting along the snow, there is now blue sky, and a sun that is getting quite hard on the eyes. But it seldom gets warmer than 20 degrees below. This is the coldest month of the year in Foxe Land. At the moment it is quite a bearable cold.

The days are slipping by at an amazing speed. The alarm clock wakes me at 7 A.M. and in an incredibly short while it is bedtime again. The fixed events of the week, such as Friday night and the Northern Messenger, and Sunday seem to pass like milestones beside the Flying Scotsman. We have both cut off all our hair. Mine should have reached a reasonable length again by the time the ship calls, but I am in no hurry to leave. I am exceedingly content here.

Very little has happened to break our routine. One day I went out to Tesseyoumajuak with the dogs and spent a rather embarrassing hour trying to make conversation with two Eskimo women. It was a beautiful day and the dogs were going like the wind.

We stopped to look at some traps on the way back. The only way to halt the sledge was to turn it over. When we turned it right side up it was off like a cork from a bottle. I lost my seat twice and had to race after it. I carried my long trapping knife as if it was a red-hot poker, to make quite sure that I did not fall on it, if I tripped.

An old Eskimo brought a hare in to trade one day and treated me to a long harangue about Jesus and God, and, all in the same breath, told me the cold wind came in at the bottom of his pants and made his knees sore. I gave him something

101

for his knees. Yesterday the natives brought in a red fox, a real old English Reynard, nearly twice the size of the white ones.

February 6th–19th.

We have had another visit from old Saila. He came in to trade and brought some ivory with him. He had travelled all night by moonlight and was tired. He unwrapped his ivory, polished it and set it on the table: two carved caribou. Then he drank his tea and fell asleep, snoring rhythmically. He traded his foxes, shook hands gravely, and took his leave. As his sledge grew smaller and smaller in the distance we could distinguish his grave upright figure from his two sons: a king among his kind.

On Saturday (11th) there was a blizzard accompanied by bitter cold. Old Tudolik came in to trade. He was so cold that he shook like a dog. He traded and drank the tea we gave him. Half an hour later we found him digging among the empty cans in the rubbish barrel, like one of the bears at Jasper.

Next morning a team appeared at breakfast time; it was Neencaksie and his mother. They had given up in the blizzard the previous evening, unable to carry on farther and thinking themselves lost. Next morning they had crawled out of their snow house to see the flag-pole above them, and the Post only two hundred yards away. We gave the old woman some food to take with her, and she thanked us in a noisy incantation.

On Tuesday Chesley left us to go inland. It was a bitter day. It grew so cold in the afternoon that I had to sit in the kitchen. I thought of Chesley on the sledge and pitied him. He was only about three nights absent. The going, he said, was excellent though the cold bitter. The frost got at the dog's feet and made them bleed. It balls between their paws and they tear it out with their teeth.

On Saturday I went hunting in the afternoon. It was a beautiful day. There was a great number of weasel tracks about.

In one place there were four weasel tracks round a lemming burrow. Poor little lemmings! They belong to that unfortunate strata of the animal kingdom, the base line, the staple food of the next most numerous animals.

I had just climbed a hill and was looking at the view when Otoochie's little son popped up over the crest. He was following a hare track. He beamed and beckoned me to follow. He looked so quaint, a little hooded figure with a long gun over his shoulder, held by the barrel. His face flushed brick red with the cold, and the neat, bobbed fringe of his black hair showing beneath his hood. His eyes beamed from under the fringe. I followed his two short chubby legs in sealskin boots twinkling along, up and down hill.

The hare had done a series of figures of eight. We had rounded a rocky slope when it rose up before us and loped off. I landed a bullet in front of it, and it stopped and sat up with a foolish inquiring look. A great woolly object that looked as if it had come out of a pantomime.

The boy was down on one knee and, as I looked back from him to his target, a puff of snow flew a few inches to the side of the hare. The hare loped off, looking very much affronted. Its lolloping back view expressed aggravation. It stopped and looked round disapprovingly. I fired, and my bullet kicked up the snow beside him; this time he was off in real earnest.

Farther on we met Otoochie. He was standing on the skyline against the cold orange light of sunset. His hood was thrown back a little and as he stood there, he seemed the relic of some ancient creation in that silent wilderness. The image of man as he was first created, primeval and eerie.

"There is my father", said the boy and the spell was broken. Otoochie descended the slope; he was beaming and blowing out clouds of tobacco smoke. I lent him my gun and he wandered off with his son, on the trail of the hare. These two squat, furry figures receded in the distance, the picture of contentment. They are devoted to each other. Both happy boys in mind.

103

February 20th–25th.

We had one day of brilliant sunshine in the week. I took my rifle, shouldered my sealskin bag with the long snow-knife in it, and set off for the traps. The sun was so brilliant that it hurt the eyes. There was nothing in the first trap. The snow plate was frozen hard and had thickened. I had to remove it and find a new one. It took some time to find the proper snow to cut a new one.

Anywhere else but the North there is only one kind of snow, just snow. Here there are innumerable kinds. There is the hard firm snow that you saw or cut with a knife to make your snow house. The crisp snow that you fashion into a plate to cover your trap and then scrape so thin that it looks like tissue-paper. There is the soft mowya that clogs the runners of your sledge and wears down men and dogs. There is sastrugi, when the snow lies in hard patches furrowed and fluted by the wind, like ribbed sea sand. It was sastrugi that hampered Captain Scott's sledges and contributed to his heroic failure to return from the Pole.

There are countless other kinds and you may meet with them all in a small compass. Mowya in the valleys, sastrugi on the flats often so hard that you do not even leave a track, and drifts where your knife sinks crisply and evenly.

So it was that day as I crossed the miniature mountain range which separated the first trap from the next two. There were a few hare tracks. Two miles away out in the straits, a patch of open water smoked furiously. The vapour from the open water hung in a long pall down the straits. There was nothing in the two traps. A hare had just missed one of them; he never knew how lucky he was. The next trap was perched on a little rock in the middle of a lake, under the shadow of a high mountain. It was not only empty; there were no tracks round it, either.

I moved down the steep, sloping snow banks into a valley. I fired just one shot into a snow bank, and then a whole fusillade to test the sights of the rifle. The empty shells which I trod into the snow made little black punctures in the whiteness. The sights have not been the same since the dogs overturned the sledge and bolted downhill with it. The rifle had been packed on top. Otoochie had spent an hour or so trying to mend it, but it was not right yet.

I turned my steps up the valley. I was facing the big mountains at the bar. The sky was chilly blue but the snow was a blinding, hard white. Every drift and rock threw a clear-cut shadow. Crossing the small lake I opened the long snow gully at the bottom of which Otoochie's tent lies. On the side of the valley the sun touched a little projection of hard snow. I wondered if I could hit it. My bullet struck far above it, but at the crack of the rifle a great bird rose. It was a giant snowy owl, the bird that we always hoped to see at Elsfield, my home in Oxfordshire. It was white as the snow itself. Its great bulk and weird face gave it an unearthly appearance. I followed its flight until it disappeared, and then trotted down the valley on the hard packed crust. Otoochie said that he was sorry that I didn't shoot the owl. "They are good eating", he said. Only two other birds stay on through the Baffin Land winter; the ptarmigan and the raven.

8

THE INLAND TRAIL AGAIN

February 28th–March 4th.

ON the last day of February Otoochie and I set off inland.
We left in the still darkness of the early morning. There
was not a breath of wind. At Tesseyoumajuak we stopped to
disentangle the traces. The dogs sat or lay, their breath rising
like a smoke, in the flaming orange dawn. By midday we were
well up in the mountains of the Kidlapike Range. The sun was
blinding and very tolerably warm. We boiled some water and
made coffee, and drank it in the open. The hot coffee dissolved
the nobs of ice on my moustache.

Late in the afternoon we reached the watershed, high up in the
mountains, and then began to descend. Two gaunt glittering sun-
dogs took their station on either side of the sun. The sun paled to
yellow and drew the light away with it as it sank behind the hills.

Well out on the plain we built a snow house. The dogs got
an extra big feed, three-quarters of a sack of walrus meat. This
long travelling—nearly eleven hours a day on snow like iron,
covered with two inches of mowya—is hard on them.

Next morning we overslept. It was a quarter to eight before
we were off. The dogs got slower and slower. Red flecks showed
in their paw marks. We found two foxes and a hare in the traps.
Never had we known it so warm on the plain. There was not a
breath of wind. You do not feel the silence. Your deerskin hood
rustles at every movement making a ceaseless accompaniment.

We reached a snow house of Chesley's as it was getting dark.
The dogs were desperately tired. The longer light had enabled
us to do in two nights a distance that three months ago had
taken nearly four. But it was hard work. We were glad to get
into the snow house. A slow and biting East wind had got up
with the darkness.

Inside the snow house we sat on the bearskins and toasted ourselves. Otoochie took his long snow-knife and chopped up the hare we had taken from the trap that day. Limb after limb he chopped away, then peeled off the skin with the soft white fur on it. He would hold up a piece for me to look at and show me the fat on it, before he tossed it into the cooking pot. The snow house filled with steam, and only the glowing points of Otoochie's cigarette, the candle, and the claw-like flames of the Primus were visible. The walls dripped, but it was gloriously warm. Then the steam dissolved, objects swam back into vision and the hare was boiled or partly so. Otoochie offered me a dripping fragment that was so hot I dropped it, and picked it up covered with snow crystals. It was so tough that it was like eating a sealskin boot. I gnawed assiduously and then turned my attention to ship's biscuit, and emptied a package of raisins. By no means high feeding, but at any rate more familiar.

Otoochie continued with the hare. He had the same look of quiet determination that a dog has with a bone. He ate an enormous quantity of it. I was interested to see what would happen to the rest. Next morning I saw Otoochie cramming it into the empty raisin carton and an empty sugar pack. He would take it to his wife and children and they would chuckle and gnaw at it, while Otoochie would sit back and beam.

I was the first one to wake up in the morning. I lit the candle and the Primus. In the cooking pot embedded, in the solid chunk of ice that filled it, was Otoochie's fur cap. It had fallen off his head as he slept and into the pot before the water had frozen. The light woke him up. He looked round sleepily, felt his head all over with a look of childish bewilderment. Then his eye fell on the cooking pot. He made little sounds of dismay. I began to laugh, and as it is the rule with the Eskimo that if a man is happy one must do nothing to interfere with his happiness, he laughed too. Then he shook out the block of ice and chopped it away from the cap. The fragments were replaced in the pot and the porridge boiled.

It was colder and dark when we started. In one trap we

Harnessing the dogs to the loaded sledge

The author on the overland trail on the return journey from the Foxe Land treasure hunt

This large snow house, made up of three smaller houses each connected with the other, belonged to the Eskimo, Old Saila

Getting ready to leave the previous night's snow house in spring sunshine

The author wearing goggles as a protection against the spring sun

found the remains of a hare, beside it the castings of a great snowy owl. For the first time in our inland travelling we really got a view. Mile upon mile of flat snow, broken by tumbled heaps of rocks covered with snow. To the North lay a long low chain of hills.

The dogs turned their bleeding feet for home. By the afternoon we were travelling dead slow. Several dogs were going on three legs. Otoochie was using the whip, and they were getting whip-shy, crowding away to one side whenever either of us jumped off the sledge. Poor souls! They were suffering and could go no faster.

We travelled the clock round, but for a quarter of an hour. We travelled until the light failed and plodded along through the dusk. The moon came out and turned the snow to golden-white, the colour of a polar bear's fur. We both had to plug along on foot. The dogs could only just pull the sledge. At last we found that familiar round hump of snow for which we were looking. The dogs were absolutely finished. We gave them all the rest of the dog-feed. We were tired ourselves. We ate our stew and tumbled into our bags. All next day we slogged through the hills, and it was dark when we passed under the flag-pole into the Post. Three nights for a trip that took six in midwinter.

March 5th–19th.

I arrived back just too late to miss a rather intriguing incident. Down the coast live two Eskimos, in the same camp, called Atchelak and Tunidlee. From the version that was laid before Pitsulak, Tunidlee forced Atchelak's daughter to drink so much water that she had died in convulsions.

Pitsulak had run into the camp with a dog team a few days later to be accosted by Atchelak, who apprised him of a plan he had made. Nobody but an Eskimo would have divulged his plan, but they cannot keep anything to themselves. He planned, so he said, to stun Tunidlee with a club and then drop him through the ice.

113

The wily Pitsulak listened and smiled; he knew white men and Eskimos sufficiently well to see a bloodless solution to this. Professing deep interest and sympathy in Atchelak's cause he persuaded him to come into the Post and bring Tunidlee with him on some pretext, and get the white men's advice on the matter. In they came and thrashed the whole matter out with Chesley. Atchelak, at first adamant, finally decided to forgive Tunidlee. Tunidlee, at first brazen, broke down and wept at the state his soul must be in, and to think how he had prejudiced his chance of eternal salvation. He wept all night and kept Chesley awake to such an extent, that he tumbled out of bed again and gave Tunidlee two biscuits to quiet him down. Next day all three set off down the coast together.

The sun is getting blinding bright now and on the mildest days it thaws at noon. On Monday the 13th I took my small rifle and set out round the long trapline. It was a perfect windless day, and so bright that I was sorry that I had left my sun goggles behind. The snow was hard, with just a thin film of mowya on it to show tracks. I got to the seventh trap, the one beside the whale's drum, in good time and determined to explore.

From that trap to the bar runs a tall steep hog's back, sinking sheer into the water of the channel opposite the Post. As so often happens in this formation there is a long level ledge, fifty yards wide, running the whole length of the hog's back. The mountain side rises nearly sheer above the ledge, which lies flat and smooth like a highway along its side; below the ledge, the ground falls away in a rough and rocky hillside, in places sheer but in places easy enough to walk up. All the hare tracks that I had ever seen on the flats below, led upwards to this ledge, and it was with the feeling that I was on the verge of effecting a coup that I climbed an easy slope and found myself on the ledge. I had my ·22 rifle, ideal for rabbits and ptarmigan, but a pea-shooter against a polar bear. And it looked rather a beary place.

I walked along the outside edge and looked for tracks. About a hundred yards away I found one. The maker of the tracks, a hare, was sitting in a niche in the cliff wall and took to his heels without ceremony. I just missed him as he ran; the bullet must have clipped the hair on his back. He stopped and sat at about 250 yards, too long a shot for my little rifle, but I tried it and watched the fat woolly body lollop off. I got another hare farther on. He was sitting on a rock, hunched in a neat round ball. His small black eye showed like a black currant in a round white pudding. I tumbled him off the rock at 77 yards, paced. About half a mile beyond I came on a shed caribou antler. I chopped it out with my snow-knife. Plants had grown over the antler, which must have laid there a long time, because the Eskimos have shot out all the caribou that used to browse in hundreds near the Post. You have to track over two hundred miles farther on to find them now. I got back to the Post, very hungry, for luncheon. I never knew that a hare could be so heavy.

On Friday evening Nielson, the Protestant missionary, arrived on his annual trip from Lake Harbour. A strange little man, squeaky-voiced and shy, but possessing great courage and resolution, and a noted traveller. He was just one of those many sturdy missionaries dotted about the North. He had done the trip in six nights. One of the nights he had spent with Tunidlee, and he reported that gentleman as being very worried about his soul.

On Sunday morning we had a Communion Service. There were present myself and Chesley, sitting on chairs by the stove and nearly roasted; Echalook, who is half-witted, sitting on the slop pail; Otoochie and wife, and Koanoo, our grubby little domestic helper; Tookeke, one of the best hunters on the coast, and Pudloo, one of the laziest of all Eskimos.

The preacher wore a dirty white cassock from which his sealskin boots protruded at the bottom. Last but not least was the magnificent old patriarch Shorti. He is the lay catechist and assistant to the missionary.

The service began. Chesley and I sang the hymns in English, but everybody else sang in Eskimo. Shorti read the Lesson in

Eskimo and then expounded it. It was a Lesson from Luke about the man who was ordered to go and loose the colt and to say, if he was resisted, that the Lord had need of it. Shorti changed the colt into a dog team. The Eskimos listened attentively. Then we received the Bread and Wine, myself first. When it came to Echalook's turn he took the bread and said thank you for it. His feeble mind was wandering. He was a complete stranger to all the proceedings and thought that the bread was a small gratuity from the Company. The wine went the round; it was poured from an old medicine bottle into a battered chalice.

Then came the great moment in an Eskimo service when the congregation prays extempore. First Shorti prayed loudly and lengthily. Then Tookeke, the hunter, prayed. Koanoo who was next to him sat mute. Then Pudloo, the lazy, rambled off in prayer in a fluent, oily voice. Wakta and Otoochie remained mute and motionless. Echalook, the half-wit, sat with his head slumped forward and his feet thrust out, deep in witless lethargy. Then it was over. The Eskimos, who had been stuffy in their heavy deerskins, shook themselves like dogs, wrung the parson's hand and filed out.

March 20th–27th.

Nothing happened all the week that could be called a happening. Old Nielson got back on Sunday morning. He blundered in covered with frost and ate four separate meals. The service he held in the evening was just as intriguing as the previous one. Shorti preached at length about the widow's two mites. He used the word *kenowya*, meaning a trade token. The Eskimos rather lost the point of the parable as the two tokens seemed quite a respectable sum; it would buy two pounds of flour. But they listened most attentively. The missionary said that they prayed endlessly at his services at the camps. They pray for us, and they pray for their dogs, as the dogs can't pray for themselves. We sat up late, talking, and persuaded the missionary to drink some hot whisky toddy. He choked and spluttered and beamed at us, and I think enjoyed himself.

March 28th–April 2nd.

I left early to go inland, Chesley and the missionary were rather surly at having such an early breakfast. The going was excellent and the sun quite warm. In the mountains we met Kavavou, and later we met Pingwaktuk and Aggeak. We had midday tea together in an old snow house. Kavavou left us and branched off for Noovoughdyuk up on the Foxe Channel coast. We got right through the mountains and on to the plain in daylight. There was a fox in one of Chesley's traps. He bit through my sealskin mitt, but I had prudently withdrawn my fingers inside.

We travelled for twelve and a half hours and camped for the night in a snow house that we found. We were just ready to get inside it when Pingwaktuk and Aggeak came up. We all fed together and I had to play host. Two cans of beans and hard tack with black tea made a noble meal. Pingwaktuk and Otoochie both had sleeping-bags that we had given them. Poor little Aggeak, who is only a boy, had nothing except a dogskin to lie on. I asked him if he had nothing else, not even a lemming skin. Otoochie and Pingwaktuk roared with laughter. Even when they had quieted down they kept exploding with chuckles until they were asleep. Aggeak lay down on his dogskin and prepared to make the best of it. I had a spare dicky in my bag and I gave it to him to lay over himself. I half-smoked a cigarette and gave it to him to finish. His eyes twinkled at me like a grateful dog.

Next morning it was snowing and so mild in the igloo that the metal did not even hurt my hands as I lit the Primus. I spilt a great quantity of coal-oil over my sleeping-bag. We had a huge brew of porridge. I saw that little Aggeak had a full meal, at any rate; it would be some time before he got another.

It grew colder and windy as the day went on. We travelled hard and fast on the good going. We picked up two foxes on the

117

way. I put on my snow-goggles. The glare from the snow is
deceiving. Like the African sun it is as dangerous on a dull day
as on a bright one. By evening we had covered an almost record
distance. I fed the dogs; the bags were so heavy that I had great
difficulty in lifting them. The dogs stood round vibrant with
eagerness. They could not understand why I was so slow; con-
cern showed on their wrinkled faces. At last I got the sack open
and tottered backwards with it scattering meat all over the
snow.

It took a long time to build the snow house; the snow itself
was not very good, and a wind got up.

The next day started mild, but as evening drew in a very
cold wind sprang up. We were in the mountains when darkness
fell and it was bitterly cold. We had a novel night's shelter.
There was an old snow house so buried in a drift that only the
top was visible. We cut a hole in the top, climbed down inside
and filled up the hole we had made. It was exactly like being in
a rabbit burrow, but it was wonderfully snug when we got the
Primuses going, the candle lit, the bearskins down on the floor,
and our supper cooked.

Next day we had a mere half-day's run into Dorset but the
going was so hard on the snow-slopes that it was really dangerous. The sledge went so fast that we caught up to the dogs and
passed them, and the pull from the bridle turned the sledge
broadside. To be rolled on by one of those heavy sledges is no
joke. We were home by lunch-time with a rather damaged
sledge and two dogs going loose, one trailing a broken trace,
the other having slipped her harness.

9

COASTAL JOURNEY

April 3rd–23rd.

ON Monday Otoochie and I started on the great trek for Lake Harbour. It was mild and clammy as we pulled out. We all shook hands and until we rounded the little headland, where the flag-pole stands, Chesley and Otoochie's family were waving—even down to the fat baby in the hood.

We reckoned on being away for three weeks. There was a thick fog all day and the weather remained mild and clammy. The only sign of life we saw was a fresh sledge track off the mouth of Andrew Gordon Bay. Otoochie said it was Tukuktuk's; that bad-tempered old gentleman had apparently been hunting at the floe. In appearance he is a monument of senile jollity but in reality a hard-hearted old ruffian. Last year he destroyed Etengat's nets with a harpoon.

It was nearing 6 P.M. when we approached the low headland beside which lies Ikkeashuk, the camp where the best of our hunters live. The dogs went off like a hurricane through the rough ice, and did not stop until they arrived in front of Pitsulak's big snow house. Pitsulak was the first to welcome us, then all the other hunters, all the women, and scores of little children.

Pitsulak took all our baggage into his snow house. His wife, Pouta, was there, and his small son, on whom he dotes, was sitting in her hood wearing a little deerskin suit; a perfect Eskimo in miniature. Pitsulak had two daughters; one of them, a grown-up girl, was wearing beautiful beaded clothes.

There were also strangers in the camp. Santayanna, Tom Manning's henchman, was resting before setting out on his long journey back to Hantzsch River. Tunidlee was sitting in a snow house, still very worried about his soul. He is fortunate to be still alive after Atchelak's planning to kill him. There was a pack of enormous dogs lounging about, the biggest I have ever seen.

The highlight of the whole scene was two little polar bears. They were, as Pitsulak explained, a boy-bear and a girl-bear. Putoguk had shot their mother. The girl-bear lay curled up in Putoguk's snow house asleep, while a silent gallery of Eskimos looked on. Still very white and clean, she slept with nose pillowed on one woolly leg. She stirred and opened one clear eye and then with a gentle grunt went off to sleep again. The boy-bear was in a snow house of his own. He had slept at Pitsulak's, but his snores made the baby cry and a huge snow tabernacle had been built for him. In this large chamber the boy-bear, his head too big for his body, sat looking moodily at his paws. Tiny as he was, his legs were thick and firm and his claws long and polished. In this large chamber was a solemn gathering of Eskimos. They were silently regarding the bear, all except Santayanna who was contemplating a picture of Queen Mary with the deepest gravity. It was from a magazine that he had been given at the Post.

We strolled back to Pitsulak's snow house. There was a sledge coming up through the ice. It was Kootoo returning from hunting at the floe; he had two seals and a square-flipper. The square-flipper is a large variety of seal, from which kayaks are made. That night we talked and smoked by the light of the seal-oil lamp. Otoochie crept out to visit the other snow houses. Pitsulak and I lay on the deerskins, and smoked in the dim warmth. Pitsulak has lost three boys already and is desperately trying to rear this one. Like all Eskimos he longs for a grown-up son, a companion on the trapline and at the floe, a provider for his old age. We talked until we were drowsy. Pitsulak stumbled out to round up Otoochie. Pouta rocked the sleeping boy and smiled at me. Her smiles lit up her face with a flash of radiant beauty as she looked at him. All that humanity knows of tolerance and wisdom seemed enfolded there. Pitsulak returned with Otoochie and we prepared to sleep. I chose a strategic position with my head beside the seal-oil lamp.

Spring comes slowly to the Far North

Making seal nets in the spring

Pingwaktuk (whose name means "he plays") shooting at a seal

Dogs on the edge of a floe, watching a seal coming to the surface

Watching for a seal on the trip to Nottingham Island

The next day, Tuesday, we were up and away early. Pitsulak came a little way with us. As the sun rose it brought with it a little light snow. At midday we reached the desolate camp of Acheaktooloulevik, a deep cleft in the rock, in the centre of which was an old whale-boat painted black. There was also a kayak. Higher up in the cleft were three snow houses. The dwellings were all under the snow but the porches were clear. In them were stuck the harpoons, fish spears and ice lances of the tenants.

The inhabitants swarmed from their subterranean dwellings. There was clearly something in the air. We shook hands all round before I produced a parcel from Chesley for the old woman of the camp. I called her name. There was a torrent of lamentation as if I had pulled the string of a shower-bath. She had died ten days before. It was embarrassing. A light snow began, the tension eased and people began to move about.

I began a laboured conversation. Otoochie shook hands cordially with the medicine man, Allariak, who was said to have murdered his wife's brother; then he disappeared below ground. It was useless to try to hurry Otoochie. I talked to Allariak, who had sore-eye and many troubles besides. He said that there was no tobacco or tea in the camp and that they were all hungry.

Otoochie bobbed up again and we started off. "They are not hungry," he said, "They have three walrus there. I saw them."

We went about two miles, and when we stopped to make tea, a team caught us up. It was Ooshooweetok with five thin dogs. He had come to show the way through the rough ice in the middle of the Inlet. It never freezes completely here owing to the strong tide. The ice for several square miles was composed of loose pieces frozen together and presenting the appearance of an enormous ploughed field with furrows six foot deep. We shifted half our load to Ooshooweetok's sledge. Just as we started an old raven flapped by; it was a bad omen, a damned bad one. . . . It took five hours' pushing, lifting, sweating, cursing and praying to get the sledge through the tumbled

125

masses and the flat stretches of doubtful thickness. When we did get through, the dogs started fight after fight out of pure relief.

At 7.30 P.M. we camped. The sun went down, in the centre a mighty cross. As Ooshooweetok lifted the first heavy snow block the last rays caught it and showed it white against the greying background. We dined nobly that evening on boiled deer-meat. The moon rose bright red with a curious aura round it. We were sleepy and happy. Ooshooweetok's entire luggage was a small dogskin, and I gave him my dickies to put over himself.

Next morning we left him. It was cold when we harnessed our team but a gorgeous sun came up. Only once did we come on bad ice. At midday we cached a bag of dog-feed for our return trip. There were quite a few fox tracks.

We were among the islands. All day we were threading the channels between them as we had threaded them by motor-boat last summer. I did not recognize for certain any single place on the route.

We ran into Amadjuak camp at half past seven in the evening. Three snow houses huddled in a little nook on the shore. Old Kovianuktuk escorted us into his dwelling, a skin tent blocked with snow on the outside. Light came in through a window made of seal's intestine. The house was grubby but fairly warm.

I opened the box of rations. I had brought flour and baking powder, sugar, tea, tobacco and matches for each family. We talked far into the night. The seal-hunting was good, apparently. Otoochie gave him the news. The bears at Ikkeashuk, the drowning of Pingwaertok while trying to retrieve two seals he had shot, the state of the going, the scarcity of foxes. It was a pleasant evening. The old woman nodded and the two little boys watched us intently.

Next day we pushed off taking Ikkedluak with us for a guide. Otoochie was now in unknown country. From the map of Baffin Land it looks a simple enough task to run down the floe ice close to the coast, but it isn't. We left Amadjuak camp expecting to meet a police patrol from Lake Harbour who, we knew, were due to cross somewhere about here.

We had travelled for nearly two hours when both teams set off at full gallop and brought us to a small igloo. I banged on the roof. A sleepy voice told me to come in. I found Mac and Seeootiapik still in their blankets and very sleepy. We made tea and ate some biscuits and talked and smoked. Then the door was moved and Otoochie peered in, beaming. In he came and brought Ikkedluak with him. They got a mug of tea and biscuits.

We parted half an hour later. A warm wind which had sprung up blew in our faces. It also blew the snow like soft sugar twinkling with the colours of the spectrum. It condensed on us and soaked us. It covered our loads on the sledge, then melted and soaked them too. The mud on the runners on the sunny side softened and left long dirty streaks on the snow, even though we lay on our faces on the sledge for long stretches and flipped snow on to it.

We stopped to make tea beside a *skukpaw*, a place where the sea never freezes. This one was a long channel, a patch of black, rippling water about 150 yards each way. At one end the ripples foamed under the ice like a mill-race. It seemed strange and unaccountable to find water existing in this frozen world, and harder still to remember that the miles of floe, like a vast white prairie, have fathoms of water below them.

The wind was warm when we started again, and the ground was hidden in a swirling soup of snow. The dogs had it right in their faces; we stopped, covered the soft runner with wet snow, and managed to freeze it on. It was dark and very much colder when we reached Etonnik. The water and snow had frozen on us solidly. Our baggage was cased in ice.

There was an enormous turn-out to see us arrive; scores of hands to shake and scores of small children to climb on the sledge and chase each other round it. We put up at the abode of Shorti, the patriarch, who was away. His wife, a little, wrinkled old woman, was a wonderful hostess. In no time she had taken away our wet clothes and hung them up to dry. As many of the population as could push their way in, did so. They regarded us with a silent, unwinking stare. Otoochie regaled them with the news. Sakiassie, one of our hunters, was there. He said he had been so hungry that he had had to leave his traps and come down to Etonnik. I gave him some tea, tobacco, and biscuit and told him to go back again.

Next morning we set off with Kotkchaluk to guide us. It was blowing like a fiend, head on. All day we wrestled with the land crossing. This consisted of climbing one big river between high mountains to its source and descending a smaller one on the far side. Wind had whipped the snow off the frozen cascades and left a great stretch of blue-green ice, slightly convex in shape. So strong was the wind that it was almost impossible to stand upright against it. The dogs slipped, sat down and slid back. For hours we stumbled and slithered on in this way.

It was getting late when we reached the top of the watershed. The stream we followed down now flowed in a narrow crack. In places the snow had drifted in deeply and made our progress very slow. The stream ended with a very deep fall, down which we went as if down a toboggan slide. We decided not to face the shore ice at that stage of the light but to unharness the dogs and run up a snow house. We had a very large meal, and Koktchaluk looked as if he had never tasted food before. He was not very communicative.

Next morning the wind was still blowing in billowing white clouds from the exposed hillsides. It covered the dogs' faces as if it were thick white soup. On the side of the Bay opposite to that where we had camped was a native camp, which Otoochie wanted to visit. As he usually has some purpose behind such requests, I let him. The first snow house we went into contained a woman and her family, lying in bed, naked as they were born. The woman came to life in an instant and called on her family to look at the white man. Hanging up on the tent-pole was a picture of the children of the Governor of the Hudson's Bay

Company. "They are beautiful, aren't they?" said the woman. Indeed they were.

Otoochie had a letter for her, a piece of paper covered with syllabics folded and refolded until it was about two inches each way and then tied with ribbon. We delivered a letter to the other snow house. There, too, the family was still in bed and the mother delightedly called to her children to look at me. They, too, were naked and unashamed.

Our guide left us here. The mud was coming off his sledge-runners, and he wanted to get back to his camp. Eskimos hate to be away from their own people.

We pushed on, with the going very difficult indeed. Somehow or other Otoochie's belt fell off. He ran back a little way to look for it but he could not find it. On the land crossing we met Shorti returning from Lake Harbour with one of our Eskimos, Kingwatchiak. We had a very uncomfortable cup of tea together, in a high wind. It was the last bad crossing but one, and there were some very steep hillsides to negotiate.

When we emerged on to the floe we felt we were nearing our journey's end. In front of us was that long, steep coastline of Big Island which runs to the mouth of Lake Harbour Inlet. The dogs seemed to feel that they were getting somewhere at last, and made a good pace along the floe ice. Twice they dashed away at the top speed, almost overturning the sledge, only to stop on a hillock of drifted snow and dig frantically. Then Otoochie would leap into the midst and jump until the snow crust gave under him and he was standing on the ice below, waist deep in a little chamber which smelt strongly of seal.

It is here that the young seals are born. They stay here during the short period of a week or so as a white-coat. On our journey we must have burst open some twenty-five of these dwellings, but we did not find a single baby seal.

A little further on we met an Eskimo called Towky. He shook hands and smiled and then we all became embarrassed and looked at the ground and could think of nothing to say except "good-bye."

It was about 6 P.M. when we saw a very big team being driven towards us at top speed. It soon caught us up. It belonged to Tootweeya, the Company's dog driver from Lake Harbour. He had travelled hard and fast. Having left Lake Harbour early that morning he had overshot us; when he found our tracks he turned and chased us along the floe. He had an urgent message for me from the Post Manager of Lake Harbour, telling me to make all haste there, to stand by for vitally important radio message, expected in two days' time.

We went on as far as we could that day and then squashed up in a tiny igloo on the floe. We chatted till late, about how many foxes we had caught, and exchanged the news.

We awoke to a perfect morning. It was Sunday, April 9th, and Easter Day into the bargain. We were away early and driving down the floe basking in sunshine. The inevitable happened. The sun that warmed our faces melted the mud on the runners and we lost it all.

An hour later we were pushing through the shore ice on to the land, where the going was tricky. In parts it was hair-raising! We coiled the whip and put it on one of the runners to slow us up on the steepest grades. When the incline was against us we staggered and sweated and prodded the sledge uphill. We came to a little hollow in the hills where the sun was striking so warmly that patches of ground were showing through the snow. What was also showing were two fat white ptarmigan.

We stopped the sledge and snarled the traces round boulders. Otoochie lugged his heavy rifle off the sledge. At the first shot one bird fell and the other took wings and settled on a snow-slope. Otoochie sat down and took very careful aim at it, for it was a long shot. The third bullet hit it. A shower of white feathers flew and the smack of the bullet against its target drifted slowly back to me. Then we were on the trail again.

At the top of a high, rocky escarpment Tootweeya held up his hand for us to stop, and came back towards us. The action held no significance for me, but a moment later Otoochie was tearing the harness off the dogs. I went to the edge and looked over. There below us, and looking as if you could lean over and touch it, was a little wooden church. On one side was the familiar shape of the Company's house, and below that, above the sea-ice, were two boats hauled up.

It was so sudden and surprising that it struck one dumb. Five minutes later the dogs had cannoned down the hillside loose, and Otoochie and I were sliding down clinging to the sledge, with our feet thrust out in front to brake. The sledge came to rest beside the back door of the Company's house. The door opened, and out came Bell and Figgures. Off came the loads and in we went.

How pleasant is the smell of indoors after a long spell of the open! How luxurious to change your clothes and wash and tidy up your cracked and bleeding face! After all this had been done, we had a luncheon of fried venison and various canned vegetables. Later, stretched in a long chair, smoking, I turned round to see the face of Kutchinaki, our leader, looking in through the window. It was a long face, beautiful and wistful. He was standing on a snow bank looking in at me. Then Otoochie passed. He was going to church, with such other Eskimos as happen to be at the Post. It was Easter Day and the missionary was ringing the church bell.

Next day the missionary and Jock the policeman came in. The latter was with me on the walrus hunt. The awaited climax collapsed. The message did not come through, the reception was nil.

Next day I spent the afternoon with Jock and ate a large meal of deer meat and vegetables, only three hours after I had eaten a very large one at the Company's. Then a hasty march back across the ice to sit over the radio again. The message arrived. A mighty anti-climax which will reverberate over the whole North! A message of good wishes from my parents!

What with the large meals we ate and the talking we did, it seemed hardly a moment until we were assembled on Thursday afternoon for a farewell service in the church. It was a very quaint service, followed by a huge meal of ptarmigan at the missionary's house. Then Friday morning hot and bright, a great shaking of hands and the missionary taking photographs. Jimmy Bell thrusting a sack of buns, just baked, and some chocolate bars on me. The missionary gave me pills and sticking plaster; the policeman ten pounds of bacon and I gave him a copy of *Dracula* and *The Three Musketeers*.

Jock and Figgures helped push the sledge to the top of the hill, and then we were off. We had no mud on our runners and we went dead slow. It got extremely warm, and we both shed our dickies and fur caps. It was glorious to have all the fun of the snow and the sledging and warmth, at the same time. But on the floe it was colder. We stopped to untangle the traces, and it was a slow and disheartening business dragging along the floe with the plain, iron sledge runners.

Finally Otoochie could stand it no longer. He put his points plainly and forcibly. Either we go to a nearby camp he knew of and get mud, or we—and he made a gesture suggestive of days of dreary plodding, with failing dogs and dwindling provisions. His gesture was so comprehensive that it suggested not only these things but falling stocks, rising prices, and news of war!

It was 4.30 P.M. when we reached the camp. It belonged to Muckickvik whom we had met a few days before. It took five hours to boil up mud in the cooking-pot and mould it and freeze it on to the runners. During this time I sat in a smallish snow house with one old and hideous woman, two married couples and two children. I was miserable, as I had given up smoking. The cooking-pot looked as if it would never be any good again, and it was long past the time for our evening meal.

We got going early the next day. We weren't sorry to pull out of such cramped quarters. Mikkajuke, one of our hosts, came with us for half a day. It was late afternoon when we got to the long land crossing. Our way lay up a narrow watercourse, against a very strong head wind. The sides of the watercourse were perpendicular, rock and snow; and the gully was about twenty-five yards wide. The wind blew down it as down a funnel

Otoochie with the white calico square used as a screen for stalking seals on the ice

Bringing a square-flipper ashore. This type of seal weighs about
800 lbs., and its skin is used for making kayaks

The square-flipper made fast by the harpoon line to the shaft stuck
in the ice alongside

Cape Dorset, early spring

and half blinded the dogs. Where the direction of the gully ran at right angles to the wind, by some unpleasing dispensation of nature the gully broadened out with gently shelving sides. The wind blew down into it as if it meant to scoop us out. As it was getting dark, we found a sheltered angle and built a snow house.

We awoke to a beautiful sunrise, and we were not long in getting to the top of the watershed. There was even less snow on the frozen river than before. It was a river modelled in glass; in blue glass, green glass, Waterford and Venice. We avoided the glare ice as much as we could, picking our way along the edge. We stopped to make tea just above the shore ice. There were high cliffs above us, perpendicular cliffs with long black stains running down them, like the stains on College Chapel at Eton.

These stains seemed to fit in with all that I had heard of pitchblende. Leaving Otoochie to boil the kettle, I made for the bottom of the nearest cliff. Climbing laboriously over some ice-hummocks I reached the rock itself. There certainly were black streaks but they didn't look half as exciting as they had from a distance. I found a loose fragment of rock and tried to break off one of these sable pieces. It was no good at all and I returned to the sledge rather ruffled.

An hour later we were bumping along the floe, looking back at the gap in the mountains, down which we had made our way with so much difficulty. On the horizon were several big icebergs, frozen in. We passed one at close quarters. It had four irregular turrets and a curious streak of dark blue about a foot in width running all around it. It looked like a child's drawing of an Eastern temple. It also looked vaguely eatable.

The sun got stronger and, of course, the runner on the sunny side began to leave long brown streaks behind it; finally it was necessary to take a knife and chop off all the mud from that runner. We arrived at Etonnik while the sun still shone and were met by Shorti and his tribe. There was a long and unhurried parley between Shorti and Otoochie. It appeared that

there was no mud nearby and that night was at hand, and so—
Shorti led the way to his tent.

We spent a pleasant evening at Shorti's. Martha, his wife,
made a great fuss of me. She gave me a piece of white whale to
eat; it was black and not very nice. Otoochie finished it covertly.
I gave them both tobacco. Just before we turned in to sleep I
squeezed out into the open and looked about me. It was a
sharpish night and the Northern Lights were blazing. The dark
forms of sleeping huskies showed on the snow. What fascinated
me was the snow houses. The glow from inside them showed as
a phosphorescent gleam. They looked like giant phosphorescent
mushrooms, and the whole prospect seemed a weird camp of
the fairies. When I went in again the patriarch was lying on his
back with his eyes shut, singing hymns through his nose.

Martha very nearly kissed me when we set off next morning;
nearly but not quite. Just as well, for she is not nearly as clean
as she is Godly. Shorti accompanied us part of the way. So did
Opaluktuk, who is going to hunt seals, and Kakayuke and his
wife who were on the same errand. We shed these companions
beside a small *shukpaw*.

There was a thick white fog over everything and we could
just discern Opaluktuk standing up keeping watch over his
team, while his companion squatted, rifle in hand, beside the
water, waiting for seal. He was behind a mound of snow,
looking for all the world like a white grouse-butt.

It was a slow job travelling; not until late afternoon did we
pass the place beside which we had had tea on our outward
journey. It was dead calm, and two seals came up to look at us.

By the time we reached the police igloo, where we had eaten
buns so joyfully, our dogs were flagging and it was nearly dark.
We fed the dogs a quarter of a mile short of the camp, and
they got snarled at the first snow house. I let fly with the whip
and just missed a woman and baby who were creeping out of
the snow house.

Kovianuktuk was his genial, philosophical self. He produced a short bow and two arrows he had made for me. We

138

spent a pleasant evening. I showed them some photographs which the missionary had developed. Otoochie failed to recognize his wife and there was a general laugh at his expense.

The white mist held next day. At times it was very cold. My beard and moustache were covered with ice. My face was so sore that it was agony to have my sun-goggles resting on the bridge of my nose. I unravelled a piece of hairy string and wrapped it round the bridge of the spectacles. This alleviated things a little. Then I struck myself twice in the face with the dog whip. It hurt like hell and stripped a lot of skin from my face.

In the course of the day we had at least twenty false alarms from white-coat seals. After a lot of galloping and sniffing and digging, all we found was the remains of a dead one on the snow. A fox had dug it out, eaten it up completely, and rolled up the skin like a sock; it was rather like a woolly bed-sock, and the skin was remarkably unspoilt. That evening it was snowing, with a S.W. wind, when we built a snow house on the floe.

Next morning it was still snowing and blowing a blizzard. We had been going for perhaps one hour when Otoochie gave an unearthly squawk, stopped and pointed, with the snow swirling round him. About 200 yards distant was an Eskimo. Our dogs turned and made for him. It was Seeootiapik, the police driver, and behind him, as we approached, was his team and Mac sitting on the sledge.

We spent half an hour together making a very uncomfortable cup of tea behind a snow-shelter. We seemed to have known each other for years and chattered like magpies while the snow filled every crevice in our garments and got in behind our goggles and obscured the view. They told us that our old crossing at the *shukpaw* was broken up now, our sledge tracks terminating in open water. An Eskimo had shown them a new and much better way.

We parted, but our own dogs were in such poor form that we went like a funeral. We travelled at little better than a walking

pace all day, and we crawled into Acheaktoolouevik, where, in
this poverty-stricken niche in the coast, we spent the night. The
dogs here had to be kept off with whips while ours were fed. It
seemed that our dogs would never finish their meal.

Snow was falling in huge flakes that lay like icy pads on our
faces. We were tired and hungry. We slept in four snow houses,
joined together and almost entirely underground. I had to go
through the connecting doors on my hands and knees. It looked
like a fairy palace that had been leased to a garbage dump and
then roughly tidied up by an army of chimney sweeps. We slept;
Amenuke, his wife, and a sick child; Otoochie and myself.
The child kept crying out with pain in the night. It was in
great suffering. The other inhabitants packed in to look at us
and tried to sell me ivory. Amenuke had constructed a model
snow house and porch out of whalebone, and an ivory Eskimo
on a sledge with one dog pulling it.

We left Acheaktoolouevik at a walking pace in deep snow.
It took us five and a half hours of solid plodding to reach
Ikkeashuk, which should have been a light airy gallop of three
hours. The population forged out to meet us; Putoguk and Par,
who were both mourning for their sins and very doleful; Noah,
who was snow-blind, instead of keeping to the friendly dark of
the snow house, came and sat on the sledge, without glasses.
He couldn't bear to miss anything! Tunidlee was there, still
worried about his soul. Most of all in evidence was Pitsulak,
the sea-pigeon.

I had one small commission and that was to look at our
boat, the *Keegarveealuk*. She was beached among the snow
houses and her deck was covered with snow. Pitsulak and I
walked back to the sledge and as we walked he tried his level
best to sell me his bear-cub. I tried my level best not to buy it
and take it back on the sledge; as we should have to sleep out
a night it seemed too bulky as a bedmate in a snow house.

We left at midday, and it became increasingly obvious that
we would not see Dorset that night. The dogs were going at a
walking pace; several of them had sore and swollen feet that

bled. The going was very tiring on foot in deep snow. The floor was a dead flat blanket of snow and the runners of the sledge looked as if they were pushing their way through angel-cake. We couldn't have gone slower if we had tried.

Samuelie and his brother caught us up in the afternoon. We had seen them at Ikkeashuk and they could not resist the temptation to chase us in. At 8.15 we had to camp and build an igloo. I had just coiled our traces up to perfection when three dogs jumped on our leader Kutchinaki. I dashed in with the bundle of coiled traces as my only weapon. By the time peace was restored once more the traces were in a hideous muddle.

We had a rare evening meal and such a one as those two brothers seldom saw. We ate up all our remaining food and cracked the deer bones for marrow. The two brothers slept huddled together; they were both very young. I threw my dickies, the duffle, and the heavy deerskin one over them. They thanked me sleepily. If they had had tails they would have wagged them.

We started off next morning in a vile cold blizzard. It was April 21st and Friday at that. At times we thought that the dogs would give up altogether. By 11 P.M. we were in sight of old Cape Dorset, crawling amidst the sea-ice. The sky was black over the open water in the strait. Our destination seemed to come no nearer. We passed Neeta, the big spring camp, and then after an age we raised Tellik and opened Porkituk inlet. Even in sight of the flag-pole the dogs would go no faster. We got into the Post, our arrival absolutely unnoticed. I surprised Chesley reading a book in the house. We had so much to talk about that we chattered incessantly until bedtime. By which time I had eaten so much that it took three days to get my digestion right.

10

TREASURE HUNT TO FOXE LAND

April 24th–May 1st.

THIS has been a week of hard work. Real hard work; packing the furs into bales, carding, stamping, with the women sewing on the big cloth labels with the address Beaver House—that murky hole in that murky street in the City of London. We then packed Tom Manning's specimens. In the middle of all this a message from R. P. saying that a permit had been taken out for me to export five live eider ducks of each species for Peter Scott. How I shall get even one I don't know, but I shall have to do something about it to justify myself. The weather has been so warm that we have gone about without mitts. The two bears are still languishing at Ikkeashuk.

The radio is dead at the moment owing to an eclipse of the sun. On Sunday morning (1st) we sat outside and sunned ourselves. There were snow-buntings hopping about and twittering. I looked up suddenly to see three ptarmigan flying overhead. Their wings flashed white in the sun like the whitest of ivory, against the deep blue. The floe edge is rapidly creeping nearer to the coast as the warm sun melts chunks off it and they drift away.

The highlight of the week was the appearance of Pitsulak with the most perfect ivory carving of myself. It is a masterpiece. He left out my beard and gave me a rather foolish smirk; otherwise it is perfect. It is now in the Scott Polar Institute at Cambridge.

May 2nd–15th.

Tuesday was the 269th anniversary of the Company's incorporation. It passed without any great celebration as we have only three-quarters of a bottle to last until the ship comes. I was busy with preparations for my forthcoming trip to the Foxe Channel coast. I have always longed to see this romantic and little-known place. Christopher D'Aeth and I used to discuss plans for leading an expedition there one day.

The purpose of this particular trip is to investigate the supposed deposit of asbestos. A sample was brought in by an Eskimo, two years ago, and sent down country only to prove of very low grade. But it showed that there was something there, and it was sufficient to stir all the treasure-seeker's passion.

On Wednesday Otoochie cut up dog-feed, and early on Thursday morning we left. It was the old trail through the mountains that has become so familiar. We saw plenty of ptarmigan tracks, but no ptarmigan. The going, though not good, was better than we expected. We left the inland trail in the afternoon and pushed westward. The mountains gave way to foothills, and then low rolling country like Salisbury Plain, and then dead flat.

We passed a pleasant evening in the snow house. Little by little I edged Otoochie on to the subject of ghosts and spirits. He told me the story of the ghost sledge which made a faint swishing sound but left no track, of the *kelliok pellik*, the water spirits who moan under the ice and who are occasionally seen in the guise of a white whale with two heads.

Then he told me of a ghost that he saw as a child. He was entering the snow porch of his father's igloo when he saw what he took to be a dicky hanging from the wall. He looked again and saw that it was a figure. Whether it was male or female he could not say. He had turned and dashed out into the open. I told him a few ghost stories to which he listened attentively but they puzzled him. They ran counter to his idea of ghosts.

We finished breakfast next morning and looked out of our igloo to see a flock of ptarmigan feeding quite close to us. I rummaged for cartridges, retrieved my rifle from its canvas case and set out in their direction. I crept along a little way and looked up to find that they had vanished. I had left my dark

The lakes thaw with the spring

Spring comes to Cape Dorset. The different Post buildings are spaced to prevent a single fire burning them down

Chesley Russell appraises the melting sea ice. The slower it melts,
the later the dreaded mosquitoes arrive

Both these photographs include a ptarmigan in its winter plumage
— almost invisible against the background

glasses in the igloo and already, in that short space of time, my eyes were watering and beginning to smart. As we harnessed the dogs a snow-bunting came twittering by. It seemed strangely unreal in this hard, white waste of plain. All day we forged along. The snow was soft and our pace slow.

In the late afternoon we came out of a slight dip to see the camp on a ridge ahead of us. Three big snow houses with ice lances stuck in them, standing out against a pale evening sky. It was not until we came to a stop beside the nearest that we saw the bay and mile after mile of rough sea-ice, piled up in blocks as far as the eye could reach, and tinged a pale orange by the setting sun. It was the Foxe Channel ice.

There was only one man in the whole camp. All the rest were hunting at the floe. The women crowded round us and shook hands. A pack of dogs nosed and snarled round our teams. Most of them were small and stunted from lack of food. They were hungry now. We had to feed our dogs in a snow porch with every living soul hard at work keeping off this starving pack. I was deeply sorry for them. Our dogs looked almost bloated beside them.

We slept in Saila's igloo. The porches were filthy and I stumbled into the carcass of a dead dog. Inside, the igloo was slightly better. But cleanliness was a neglected virtue in that home. The drinking-water was ice, brought and kept in a filthy sealskin bag. We drank it and even enjoyed it. Saila's wife was a magnificent old woman. Her wrinkled face was shrouded by long straight hair and her hands were tattooed. There were three daughters there, and her son's wife, and a baby. The baby kept on calling me father and reaching out its hands to me. The daughters looked at me from under their eyelashes, and tittered. One of the daughters was ill. I gave them the news and shared out some food. Far into the night they were thanking me. First one would take it up and then they would all join in. They were fascinated by the exposure meter of my camera and I did my best to explain its uses.

Next day was bright and warm and we set off with a light

sledge for Noovowjuak, with only our food boxes as a load. We set a straight course for Noovowjuak across the ice of Finnie Bay. We were going to visit old Kavavou, Otoochie's father. It was a long, wearisome ride in the warm sun. Nothing but hummock after hummock of ice passing slowly by. On the mainland to the east the spurs of a low hill range ran down to the coast.

Noovowjuak's camp stands about 300 yards back from the shore. It was midday when we came in sight of the igloos with a motionless group of Eskimos round them. A little boy was down at the beach to meet us hoping to ride in with us on the sledge. He touched the bounding sledge, but the dogs were at full gallop and he bounced off like a football tackler who has received a hand off.

A few seconds later I was tipped over backwards and was left sprawling in the snow while the sledge raced on. The boy and I picked ourselves up and plodded after it. He panted like a steam-engine; his legs were very short. Between breaths he found time to point out his family's igloo and to tell me that his father was hunting at the floe, and make a few Eskimo commonplaces about the weather and the ice.

As at Nuwata the men were all away except for old Kavavou and a hunter called Napatchie. We sat in a row in Kavavou's snow house. He was a cheerful, deaf, old gentleman with a rather shrewish wife. He was engaged in carving some ivory when I came in. He carved a dog team for Chesley and a number of seals. We made tea and shared biscuits round. As many as could, arrived to join in the feast. We passed round tobacco, and there were sweets for the children. The heat which we generated was so fearsome that large pieces of ice kept falling from the roof. Every time a piece fell there would be a round of exclamations; the Eskimo equivalents for "Dear me", "Just what I expected", "Tut tut", and "No wonder".

We stayed two hours and then set out for Nuwata. We got there at 6.15 p.m. As we were unharnessing the dogs we saw, far away in the distance, a mighty flock of eider duck. A flock as

dense and black as the flocks of stint and dunlin that we used
to see on the flats at Wells-next-the-Sea, in Norfolk, returning
from a flight after goose.

Next morning we set out for the treasure hunt. We took the
only man with us as a guide. Close to the camp we saw a great
snowy owl hunting for ptarmigan. That day brought some
terribly inefficient shooting. First there were the two ptarmigan
that dropped from the sky and alighted beside us. We cursed
the dogs into immobility. One of the birds was not ten feet
from them. First I missed twice and then Otoochie missed.
Then they flew a little way and he pursued and got one. Then,
a little later, one dropped from the sky and at twenty paces
distance started to call to his friends. He opened his beak and
bobbed up and down as he did so, for all the world as if he was
going to be sick. I wounded him and he flew over a ridge. I
pursued, it seemed for miles. Twice I flushed him and in each
place that he stopped there was bright blood. Then I lost him.

We made tea when I got back. Our lips were cracking with
the sun and hot tea scalded them. The spring light had come to
the land. There was glare but yet not much warmth. About an
hour afterwards, as the dogs plodded along at a walking pace,
we saw another ptarmigan. I wounded it and our guide pursued
and retrieved it. A little farther on I knocked one over dead,
but that was on a second shot.

It was 4 P.M. when we reached our objective, a small outcrop
of rock, almost islanded by the sea. We knocked off bits of rock
with a hammer and put them in a flour sack. The rocks were
certainly an original colour. They were yellow in places; in
others there were strange pock marks. We found at last what we
sought, a small outcrop of rock, bottle green in colour. We
knocked fragments off and rubbed them between finger and
thumb and sure enough they disintegrated into asbestos wood.
That was what we had hoped to find. But there seemed to be
painfully little of it.

Then we had to decide what to do next. We had only half a
bag of dog-feed and the whole width of Foxe Land to cross.

Further, we had our Nuwata guide whom we could hardly abandon. Otoochie's solution was simple. We would drop the guide at the nearest point to Nuwata and let him walk home. The guide accepted this verdict with stoicism, and we started. We did not get far before it was time to build a snow house. I left them to it and climbed a hill from which there was a wonderful view out over the sea-ice. Far out, the ice was like great discoloured cannon balls which the whalers once dreaded so much, bergs that had settled on the bottom at low tide, tumbled out, and become sounded.

A long, blue-black pall lay over the open water. I climbed down again and did my share, by unharnessing the dogs and coiling up the traces. In the snow house we had a mighty meal of deer meat; we fed our guide until he was helpless and shared out the broth from the meat in the mugs.

I threw away a piece of silver paper from a tobacco package. The guide seized it and painstakingly collected all the used tea-leaves and wrapped them up in the silver paper and bound it up with thread, as neat as a fur bale. His face wore a look of the deepest concentration and when his mouth was open and his lower lip fallen outwards, he looked more primitive than any human being I ever saw. We gave him a good feed of porridge next morning before he left, and he bade us good-bye and padded away over the snow. He carried his rifle in his right hand. In his left he clutched his package of tea-leaves.

There was a wind that day and we were soon covered with gluey snow which thawed, and saturated both our clothes and loads on the sledge, and froze again wherever we were in shadow. But we made better time than we had hoped and got a ptarmigan or two. It was getting late when we reached a little group of hills in the middle of the plain.

We halted the team in the middle and I set out with my rifle up the slope to our left to look for the owner of a fresh ptarmigan track we could see. Otoochie climbed the right-hand slope to try to locate some ptarmigan there and if possible drive them across.

152

I climbed my hill and looked back at Otoochie. Beyond the hill he was climbing was what appeared to be a big hill far away on the horizon. Imagine my surprise when I saw Otoochie waddle a few paces from the hillock on which he stood, on to the top of this imaginary mountain; with his hood thrown back he looked like a giant from a Norse Saga. I never knew until then how deceptive the Arctic light can be, though you can find the same thing in Caithness.

We quartered this miniature mountain without success. The wind was freshening and the horizon was hidden in a yellow haze. We built a most unsatisfactory snow house, and had a wonderful meal. We made a stew, to which we added two ptarmigan, salted it well and put in some rolled oats to give it body. We drank the broth in our mugs, ate the ptarmigan with our hands and fished for the slabs of venison with our fingers. I finished my ptarmigan and flung it in a corner. Otoochie was engaged with his. He looked like a great cosy squirrel eating a nut. He retrieved my ptarmigan from the corner and left it a skeleton.

It was nearly midnight when we turned in, but still bright. A slit had appeared between the snow blocks just over my head. Otoochie stuffed the skin of a ptarmigan into it; he had skinned them in one piece. The head of the bird peered drunkenly down at me. They are so white, these ptarmigan, that they make the snow look dingy; but so that their superiors in the animal world should not starve, the Almighty etched thin black lines down the quills of their wing feathers, gave them a black edging to the tails and a black stripe over the eye.

Our last half-bag of dog-feed went that night. The dogs were so ravenous that they nearly ripped the sack open to get it, and when it was shaken out it never seemed to reach the snow.

Next day it was blowing hard. The whole world was in a sticky rainbow haze of blowing snow. We were wet when we started, and soaked by noon. We made tea in an old snow house made by the Eskimos journeying between Nuwata and the Post.

Very slowly the plain gave way to the foothills and then the mountains. The dogs could go only at a walking pace. Their minds must have been on food, for as we were going down a narrow valley they turned to one side and terminated a brisk gallop at the bottom of a steep slope, whining and straining. Twenty yards or so beyond the leading dog two fat ptarmigan eyed us sleepily. I got my rifle out, tearing the canvas case badly, and emptied a box of cartridges into my pocket. We cursed the dogs into stillness and advanced. The two ptarmigan rose and with them seven others. They flew about fifty yards and landed, took one look at us and began to feed. I approached again; occasionally they would fly or run a few yards. I took thirty-two cartridges to get eight of them. The survivor spread his wings and was soon lost on the snow-slopes of the opposite mountain side. Dreadful shooting and brutal work, but both seemed defensible at the time. We needed the birds to eat. If anyone wishes to criticize, let him try shooting at dead white birds on a white background with the wind tugging and wrenching at the muzzle of a rifle with damaged sights, with fine powdery snow blowing in your face and the action of laying your cheek to the butt causing your hood to twist your goggles across your face.

It was nine o'clock at night when we saw the next covey. They were half-way up a very steep hillside, feeding on some exposed moss. I told Otoochie to go on a little way and camp and I would catch him up.

The sun was setting a fiery yellow, as I started up the slope, wondering whether I could bag the lot of them. I slipped and fell at the bottom but the excitement of the chase carried me half-way up before I realized that I couldn't get down again. The snow was iced, and by banging my heel down I could make a dent just deep enough to hold me. But there were places where the snow was like hard white marble and I could make no impression. I managed to circumnavigate these. There was a big rock just above me and I tried to get to it; then one of my mitts, which I was carrying in my left hand, slipped and slid. I watched it go.

I reached the lee of the rock and got my breath. It occurred to me to see if my rifle was choked. It was. I pushed a matchstick down the muzzle but it only pushed the plug of ice farther in. I searched my person and the lee of the rock for some instrument to force it. At last I found the stem of some last year's plant, a plant like bog myrtle which age and cold had hardened into a short, but tolerable ramrod. By delicate passes and prods with the stalk I managed to disintegrate the plug of ice. Then I tried to blow down the barrel to clean it thoroughly. It was cold by now and my lips stuck to the muzzle and my breath left a skim of ice on the metal.

Putting in a cartridge I peeped over the rock. The birds should have been ten yards away, but were nowhere to be seen. I took out the cartridge and wondered how I should get down. There was no getting past that rock and I didn't relish trying. The wind tore at me every time I showed myself above it. I saw my mitt far away at the bottom, just short of the rocks that fringed a big lake there. Patches of glare ice showed bottle green all over it and the wind chased rills of blown snow across it, twisting and dancing as they went. The sun had gone but there was a yellow glow behind the western mountains and the rest of the sky was blue grey.

There was nothing for it but to slide and try to stop before the rocks. I unloaded my rifle and sat down on the edge of the hollow that formed in the lee of my rock. Then I started. I seemed to go surprisingly slowly for about ten feet and then I was off. I was concentrating on trying to keep feet first and to keep my rifle clear of the ground. I just succeeded in doing both these things, but in what seemed an instant those rocks were flying up to meet me. I tried to brake with my heels and elbows. I might as well have tried to do it on a sloping marble slab. The friction rolled the sleeves of my dicky up to my elbows and scorched the skin off. It was just short of the rocks that my heels hit soft snow and I stopped in a series of jerks that jarred my whole body, my feet not a yard from the nearest rock.

I retrieved my mitt and set off to find Otoochie. I was rather shaken. That worthy was building a snow house. He beamed affably as I came up, and duly noted that I had shot nothing. The bottom row of snow blocks was in place already.

I had unharnessed the dogs and set about coiling up the harness, when I was roused by a mournful shriek from Otoochie. With a terrible cry he leapt from behind his barrier of snow blocks, dashed past me waving his short arms, and shouting the word ptarmigan. There sure enough was a dog eating the ptarmigan. He was a sad, white dog and on his face was the look that all dogs wear who are caught in wrongdoing. He had eaten only one ptarmigan, and he must have been very hungry. Otoochie retired behind his barricade again, carrying the ptarmigan with him. The same dog ate some sealskin lashing before I had time to coil it up. He looked terribly thin and pathetic. That was probably the last night that I shall ever spend in a snow house. We talked a little after our meal and fell sound asleep as soon as we were in our bags.

By next morning the wind had fallen. It was all known country now, our old trapping trail. The dogs could go only at a walking pace. We got very warm. Otoochie was almost black from exposure and my nose was covered with white blisters. It was midday when we reached the sea-ice and an age before we got to the rough ice on the bar, east of Tesseyoumajuak. Even in sight of home the cairn above the harbour seemed to come no nearer, and the shore ice behind us refused to recede. It was 2.30 when we got in. I lunched off a cold deer's tongue and a pound of home-made fudge, and no one ever lunched better or felt more pleasantly satiated afterwards.

On Sunday Chesley took the team and went off to the camp at Neeta. Neeta is a spring camp and they gather there for the seal-hunting at the floe. He had an arduous day. Pitsulak was at the camp and hard at work painting pictures with the paint-box and paper that I had given him. Chesley played rounders with them and came back very tired. The two young bears were there. The boy-bear is so tame that he follows Pitsulak's sledge, loose, galloping along like a little fuzzy rocking-horse.

Ptarmigan, in summer plumage, photographed by Professor V. C. Wynne-Edwards in Northern Labrador, July 1937

Polar bear photographed in Frobisher Bay by Professor V. C. Wynne-Edwards, August 1937

Geese nesting ground

Pitsulak watching skeins of geese through one of the telescopes which the old-time whalers gave to the Eskimos

Etidlooie with a snow-goose which he has shot

Two blue geese shot by Otoochie with one bullet

11

SEAL HUNTING

May 15th–21st.

A WEEK of book-work. The end of the outfit comes this month and everything has to be wound up and closed off. We stuck to it for a whole week. Otoochie disappeared to hunt at the floe each evening. One day he brought us in some seal's liver. It was very good indeed. On Saturday afternoon we all set out for the floe. We put the canoe on the sledge and straddled it. Just clear of the Post we met Pitsulak, who was bringing in my pictures. Chesley went back to trade with him. Otoochie and I went on.

The water at the floe edge was very calm; sea-pigeons and razor-bills were dotted about; an occasional flock of eider duck crossed and recrossed in front of us. Two great gulls floated screaming to and fro over our heads. I had forgotten that there were so many birds in the world.

We took up our stations at the water edge. I fired a long shot at a seal and missed. Then, as the sun was low, we made tea and ate some bully beef and bread. The sun sank lower but the light was of such an astounding clarity that we could see for miles. We moved eastwards along the floe. Razor-bills swam warily away from the edge as we approached, only to turn and look at us. Sometimes they would dive and come up a few seconds later and gaze at us in surprise, as if they expected a dip to wash out the vision of us. The dogs would turn their heads and prick their ears as we passed them. The water was like a mill-pond.

A seal bobbed up beside us as we passed, and dived again before we could get our rifles. He reappeared a long way off and Otoochie missed him twice and I once. Occasionally we would see a great square-flipper rolling over, too far to shoot at. We

161

stopped and smoked and took stock of the calm water. The
dogs sat with their ears cocked watching the birds. A noisy
string of old squaw ducks passed in front of us flying west. Six
ptarmigan making a long journey between the headlands slipped
by. The scattered razor-bills started to call to each other. Far
away behind the great field of ice and snow the sun was touching
the mountain tops. It was a perfect northern spring dusk.

We turned for home, keeping along the water edge. A great
square-flipper broke the water and set us dragging the dogs to a
halt and reaching for a rifle. He looked at us languidly, his head
like a small football. Otoochie sat down on the snow and rested
his elbows on his knees and fired. The head slowly sank and
the water darkened round it. The dogs rushed to the water's
edge and stood there crowding and peering, ears cocked and
vibrating with tension.

We unlimbered the canoe and landed it on the mill-pond
surface. As we neared the spot Otoochie laid down his paddle
and slowly raised his harpoon arm to the vertical. He poised his
arm for a second and then, with a grunt, let fly. I paddled back
while Otoochie clung to the harpoon line.

We scrambled back into the ice and beached the canoe. It
took our combined strength to haul our quarry clear of the
water. Otoochie made slits in the flippers as handholds and
taking a flipper apiece we hauled it on to the sledge. There it lay
on its back, flippers folded like a grey Crusader. A steady rill
of crimson ran from its head, as we lifted the canoe and laid it
on top of him. There was not enough lashing to encircle both
seal and canoe and we had to use the whip-lash. There was
nowhere to sit on the sledge so I stood on the bows and Otoochie
at the stern and we turned our head for home. As we had no
whip the dogs were always stopping, and we had to pelt them
with snowballs all the way home. We got very thirsty, so
Otoochie climbed into the canoe and lit the Primus. We boiled
snow and drank it. The sledge moved in a series of jerks and
bounds varied with halts when the dogs turned round and
looked at us, and I jumped off to collect more snowballs.

There were a few seals on the ice, and the dogs would some-times tear off at right angles and make for them at full gallop, with our crazy equipage rocking and swaying. The clear grey light of a spring dusk brooded over everything. The seals allowed the dogs to get within a quarter of a mile of them before leisurely plopping into their holes. It was late when we got home.

May 23rd–28th.

Another week of book-work and the excessively tiresome business of taking an inventory. A wind blew the whole week, sighing round the house. The snow is hard and lumpy and pools of water are collecting in the hollows. Etidlooie came in bringing the ivory ring he had carved for me. He had done it exceedingly well and was paid well for it. He got an old dicky and an old sweater, and went away rejoicing. Old Tudelik had a shirt of mine that was wearing very thin. "I will be saying thank you for this for a very long time", he said. Tunidlee, the alleged murderer of Atchelak's daughter, who was worried about his soul, sent me a deer's tongue by the hand of his son. We were very grateful for it.

Next day Etidlooie came in with twelve ptarmigan and we had a royal feast. There were splashes of brown plumage on the ptarmigan to show that they recognized spring was here. On Saturday a flock of snow-buntings took refuge under the lee of the house. They were hiding from some enemy who was invisible to us, probably one of the great ghostly snowy owls that never leave the country even in the winter. The snowy owl, with the ptarmigan and the raven, see the winter through, when all others have fled south.

The real event of the week was the surprising announcement that an opposition trader is to set up here in the summer. No mere adventurous greenhorn either, but a trader who was 25 years in the service of the Company, and who knows Eskimos and Eskimo trading methods as few other men alive do.

May 29th-June 4th.

Spring has made great inroads this week. Otoochie went down to Neeta with dogs to collect Etidlooie to help with the work on the Post. On his way back we saw a wild swan at the floe edge and a flight of blue geese. Natives who came in to trade brought word of geese, the advance guard of that great horde that comes to nest each year in the safety of the Barren Lands. Patches of ground, covered with last year's grass, are appearing through the snow. Water is trickling again and, above all, there is a very faint but discernible smell of moorland.

The days have been warm and blue and windless. It is light enough at midnight to read a book in bed, so light in fact that we have had to put up blinds over our windows to allow us to sleep at all. The rather wearisome task of taking sea temperature has begun again. It means wandering among the rough ice, sinking to one's knees through the rotten snow crust, to find a crack through which to lower the thermometer.

Every evening we go to the top of the hill above the Post and look at the floe edge. The sea is dotted with small pans of ice that gives a momentary impression of waves breaking at the crest before you realize their immobility.

The edge of the floe is always a different shape. Bit by bit it is breaking up and floating out to sea. There is a huge crack that shows like a narrow blue line cutting off several square miles of it.

One night Chesley and I sat on the rocks on the hill-top and watched far away the hunting of a seal. On the floe below we saw a dog team crawling along. Two figures sat on the sledge, and in front of them their dogs showed as crawling dots. Watching them idly, we saw the sledge stop and the two figures detach themselves from it, one to rummage with the lashings of the load and the other to advance on the dogs who sank into tense stillness. Through binoculars we saw the kneeling figure take off a seal screen and unfold it, while the other swayed rhythmically as he cast the long whip-lash backward and forward. The setting sun turned their figures to a shining, saffron yellow.

Beyond the sledge, and about two hundred yards distance from it, was the bolster-like figure of a seal on the ice. He was lying beside a crack, enjoying the evening sunlight that was gilding the great motionless prairie of floe ice.

The stalk began. The figure with the screen advanced and then froze whenever the seal raised his head. The approaching figure seemed no more than a few yards distance from his quarry when Chesley, who had the glasses, announced that he had planted his screen and was sitting down to shoot. He must have been close, for his aim was short. The team suddenly turned and dashed towards the kill; leaping to his feet and carrying his screen like a large, open umbrella, the hunter ran towards the seal. There was no need to hurry. It was stone dead. It was seconds afterwards that the report of the rifle drifted up as a faint pop.

On Sunday evening Chesley and I played rounders with the two Eskimo families. We played until we were dead beat. By that time Otoochie had fallen into a pool of dirty water and drenched himself to the skin, and I had bruised my heel on a rock trying to catch Chesley out. It was hard exercise.

12

ARCTIC SPRING

June 5th–11th.

MORE birds come and more ground appears through the snow. There are the great battalions of geese—Blue Geese, Greater and Lesser Snow, Canada and Brent. The floe is drifting off very fast and the large hole that has opened off Tellik is spreading to the floe edge. The eider duck are appearing in myriads and the wading birds are on the beaches.

Thursday, the real red-letter day of the month. Early in the morning we set off goose-hunting—not so early as we should have, as the two Eskimos overslept, and I had to rout them out of their blankets. We found only five dogs to harness to the sledge and with them we started off, two Eskimos and myself, with a little puppy running beside us. Nothing would shake him off.

Loons and eider duck quacked and honked. The sun shone with a beautiful dry warmth from a cloudless sky. At the open water we bore to the westerly shore and started to mountaineer over the hummocks piled on the land. There were broad fissures between the hummocks, with rocks at the bottom. The dogs toiled and panted and hung out their tongues. One of them fell down a crevasse and had to be hauled up by the harness—by no means as easy as it sounds. Then we remembered the puppy. I picked him up and carried him. With an armful of floppy plush I jumped the cracks in the wake of the sledge. It took us an astonishing time to round the glistening strip of sea that looked like a panel of shining metal.

Back on the floe, at last, we disregarded two seals lying on the ice to the east, and made for the rough ice on the bar which passes the sea into a vast inland pool between granite cliffs. At the top of the bar we saw ahead of us what looked like an

167

enormous dog team. When we had bumped and blundered through the hummocks we had leisure to look again. The dogs were coming towards us. There was no sledge and they were loose. They looked like a wolf pack, but they were our dogs who had deserted the Post to go hunting; no wonder we had only been able to find five when we started! These five looked at their erring brothers with conscious virtue.

Forward came the pack. They lolled long tongues with ingratiating smiles but their consciences were loaded with guilt. They looked like schoolboys who had got a day off from school on the pretext of illness, and had then been discovered fishing by their schoolmaster. We had no spare harnesses, but we could put two dogs to each trace, which we did. Traces were detached from the bridle and knotted, harness fashion, at the loose end. A loop was knotted half-way down and secured to the bridle. Thus we doubled our number of dogs. The rest ran with us like outriders beside a coach. They were terribly anxious to please.

Half a mile farther on occurred one of those rare and memorable occasions in life when the balance of probability is ruthlessly upset to allow a thousand to one chance. I was rolling a cigarette when a cry from Etidlooie set me staring over his head. Not twenty yards from the ground and nearly above us was a huge Canada goose, flying dead slow. It looked like a Chinese print with snowy crags behind it. I grabbed my rifle from under the lashings and jammed a cartridge into the breach. The great bird had passed us and was circling slowly back and to the side of us. As it drew level I fired and missed, and as it quartered away I fired again. It dropped like a stone with wings outstretched, its head blown clean away. As we drove on towards the shore I was wrapped in a rosy cloud of exhilaration. The feeling that Providence had singled me out to bestow a favour on me, the feeling that a glorious fluke always brings. The ice glistened and the sun warmed our faces.

It was a glorious day. As the shore drew closer we saw on a patch of gravel what we took to be a snow-goose. As we got nearer we slowed down and loosened our rifles. But it was a hare. It sat up, treated us to a long stare and sped up a rocky ridge, stopped to look at us again, to see if we had done anything while its back was turned, and then sped away out of sight.

Once on land we unloaded the sledge and secured the harnessed dogs. The others stretched out beside them. The little pup, who was worn out, fell sound asleep. We made tea and buried the goose under a heap of stones. Under another we buried all our food. It would have taken a bear to have dug them up, though the dogs probably tried hard enough in our absence. They watched us depart, rifles in hand, with drowsy contentment.

We made our way up a boggy glen. In front we could hear the cry of a goose. At the watershed was a boggy lake and on it a very wide-awake goose. We crept up in Indian file looking like three of the Seven Dwarfs. Otoochie was in front. The goose judged us rightly. He allowed us to approach, to squat down in line. Then when Otoochie, elbows on knees, raised his rifle to aim, the goose bounded clear, shaking the water from its sides and flapped away from us.

We pushed on. The ground fell away from the watershed to a large lake locked in the high mountains. Otoochie and I walked across the ice, Etidlooie went round the shore to execute a flanking movement. It was soft and tiring on that snow-packed ice, and the sun was hot. Geese were feeding in a big flock in a patch of bog, a hundred yards beyond a big rock. Keeping the rock between us and our quarry we plodded on. So complete was our cover that we adopted no caution until we quietly cocked our rifles and edged ourselves on to the sky-line of the sun-warmed granite. Otoochie fired, and I fired a second later as they rose. They climbed into the still air, the mountains throwing back their clamour, and swung past us as we lay. The sun shone on the grey and black of their wings and the shining white of the snow-geese.

We sent three heavy bullets droning through the flashing ranks, without disturbing a feather.

Otoochie had killed his goose stone dead. He had also killed another that was standing on the other side of it. We sat down and waited for our companion. A peregrine falcon had a nest in a crag on the hillside. The young ones were screaming petulantly. One of the parent birds flew over us carrying a small bird, probably a snow-bunting. The petulant screaming redoubled and then died away. Occasionally geese would fly over and we would flatten in the bog, but they never seriously thought of settling.

Finally Etidlooie appeared perspiring freely. He beamed at our two geese. Otoochie removed his sealskin pants and put the large goose into one of the legs, tied up the ends and slung it on his shoulders like a bag, and we moved on. Etidlooie got the next goose and the last. The rest would stand for no more after that. He fired first and we both pumped random shots at the retreating flock. On its back lay a white snow-goose, stone dead, wings outstretched. I photographed him beside it.

All that afternoon we wandered on sweating in the deep drifts and panting on the hillsides, occasionally sitting down to smoke and occasionally flattening ourselves as geese flew over. We saw a snowy owl, hunting, and a Greenland falcon. I told them that in my country men tame the falcon and use it to hunt birds for them. Their eyes searched my face. No, the white man was evidently not joking; then he must be telling a terrible lie. White men are queer anyway.

On one of the lakes the ice did not reach the shore on one side. The two Eskimos grinned and chuckled like conspirators. Etidlooie took a length of sealskin line and tied a stone to it and a white goose's feather. They both knelt on the edge of the ice and lowered this plummet into the depths. They watched, faces close to the water, breathing heavily.

I left them, to stalk a distant flock of geese, who allowed me to plough through two hundred yards of deep drift before taking to the air. When I returned the Eskimos announced that they had seen three fish. This seemed to please them. Apparently they had lowered their apparatus to see if there were any fish

Last of all the sea itself thaws

Husky pups enjoying the spring sunshine

A polar bear skin hung up to dry with the seal skins

The last of the ice goes out with the spring

there. The fish were sufficiently intrigued with it to come up for closer inspection. The Eskimos had the evidence they wanted. Two days later they returned with their spears, and their families, and killed twelve trout. We got to the sledge at four o'clock. The dogs looked at us drowsily. I filled the kettle from a little bubbling brook. I could hardly tear myself away from the sound, which was so welcome after months of frozen silence. There were whiffs, too, of that moorland smell, the more wonderful for being so rare; never have I felt the spring so gloriously.

We travelled back at a leisurely pace. I fell off the sledge twice. The little puppy strove manfully to keep up but he was very tired. Near the open water was a seal at the top of its hole. Otoochie fitted up his screen, the crossbars with the white cotton covering. It was a long, patient stalk and the dogs who watched his every movement were tense and rigid. Those in harness we could control, but not the loose ones. A ragged, gypsy-looking dog, a hard puller but undisciplined, broke down under the strain. He started to creep forward and then set off in a mad gallop after the seal. Otoochie saw it coming. He was not as near to his target as he would have wished, but he had no time for regrets. Planting his screen in the snow he crawled round the edge of it and took as steady an aim as time afforded. At the crash of his rifle our team bolted towards him. Etidlooie tried to leap on the sledge, hit me in doing so and bowled me off backwards. The puppy, thinking that this was a game for his benefit, tried to sink his little thorny teeth into my hood. When I rejoined the team and the two Eskimos, they were regarding the seal. A little rill of blood trickled from beside its flipper. It was stone dead with a bullet in its heart.

Sunday was the usual day of rest. Rest, in the sense that no work is done. It was a still, warm day. I picked up my heavy rifle and strolled over the hills towards the cape. The stones felt sharp through sealskin boots, but worlds better than the deep drifts of sodden snow, when you sink over the tops of your duffle stockings.

In the bay fronting the open strait the ice had all gone, but a ragged rampart of it clung along the water's edge. The water was alive with birds. Eider duck in hundreds, and king eiders too. There were old squaw ducks in separate flocks and snobbishly apart were some mergansers. A small brotherhood of gulls, kittiwakes, Iceland and herring-gulls rocked lazily on the ripples. An elderly herring-gull sat on an ice-pan, head under its wing asleep.

The sea was deep blue. The wild chorus of the birds mingled with the slapping of the ripples along the ice bluff. I could not resist shocking the sleeping gull out of his idiot complacency. His ice-pan was farther off than it looked. With the three hundred yard sight my bullet chipped away a fragment of the water-line. Flock after flock of birds crossed and re-crossed in front of me. each making their distinctive noise of alarm, wearing all the patterns of the kaleidoscope with their flashing wings.

I left them and found the cold trail of a bear near where I had been sitting. I strolled back slowly. Suddenly my eye lighted on a ptarmigan. It was a cock and still in full winter plumage. It sat on a pile of grey rocks and would have been visible at nearly a mile. The thunderous crash of cordite almost in its ear sent it scampering to the ground, to mount again a moment later to its old perch; ptarmigan can stand a lot. I laid my rifle down and felt rather ashamed. It looked reprovingly at me out of its beady black eye. Fumbling in my sealskin pouch I got out my camera. I took four photographs of it at fifteen feet, before it spread its wings and flew away scolding. It sat on a rock near the shore and continued to scold. I did not trouble it further.

Across the ice of the big fiord a heat haze hung over the Baffin Land coast. On the near side of Andrew Gordon Bay, water had eaten through floe to the granite cliffs. A team was coming down the fiord. I could see the dogs as crawling black dots, the projecting runners of the sledge, and the pointed hoods of the two Eskimos on it, both looking like midgets on

174

that white waste. It turned out to be old Pitolassie and his son, who were bringing in an ivory kayak that he had carved for me. A wonderful old warrior Pitolassie, but rickety on his legs. But once in a kayak with a paddle and harpoon, where his traitor legs can't betray him, he is as good as any man to hunt the walrus.

Otoochie and Etidlooie came trailing back that evening. They had caught twelve fish and were very sleepy.

June 12th–18th.

A week of rather cold weather. Too cold to paint. The two Eskimos have been washing and puttying the buildings prior to painting. It is warm enough in the sun but quite chilly in the shade, and the two little hooded figures move around the buildings wherever the sunlight strikes.

One evening Etidlooie brought me two pieces of rock and a lemming. One of the pieces of rock was ordinary quartz, and the other a dark form of flint of which they used to make arrow heads. The lemming was captured while they were chopping up firewood. It was an afterthought. Eskimos regard a white man who collects such things as particularly afflicted of God. But if men pay good money for rocks, spiders and grasses . . . well, they will not disappoint him! A demand always creates a supply.

One morning I was taking the sea temperature and was picking my way delicately through the ice to the land, when two great Canada geese glided over the hill behind the Post. On they came calling and chuckling, looking for a suitable place to nest. The Post buildings evidently puzzled them and they circled slowly round. The Eskimos dropped their work and called to them while I ran to the tool-shed for the shot-gun. I cannoned into my bedstead which was covered with wet white paint and had been put there to dry. By the time I emerged with the gun loaded, the two geese were winging their way across the harbour ice, calling as they went.

We are living on geese now. Twice I have come across shot-gun pellets imbedded in them. As we own the only shot-gun for 350 miles, they must have collected these pellets in the swamps of the Mississippi, in Florida, or the shores of the Gulf of Mexico.

On Saturday night the two Eskimos went off fishing again. They were back on Sunday morning with a large fish as a present for us, and a selection of gulls' eggs and one eider duck's egg. The last named was the only eatable one. All the gulls' eggs were hard set. The Eskimos went to bed at midday and slept like logs. They are helpless when they miss a night's sleep.

June 19th–25th.

This week has been a little milder. We are doing our outdoor work against time; when the flies come there is nothing to do but stay indoors and swear. There have been several days of thick mist, cutting off the tops of the mountains, the boom of the streams coming faintly through the stillness. The mist was so low one day that a merganser dropped from it and settled beside the house. Chesley went to get his gun and the merganser departed.

A boatload of Eskimos came in one day to trade. They brought sealskins and big square-flipper skins for making boots, a sealskin line, and a few small ivory carvings. They left their boat at the floe edge and walked into the Post. Ice drifted in on a south wind and they had to sleep that night penned in by the loose ice.

Our two Eskimos paint assiduously every day. The dogs cannot be kept from the wet paint; they will sleep against the walls of the blubber store, and come away coated with paint. It gives them a leprous look. Poor beasts, they are hungry now, as it is hard to get seals for them. They are starting to fight again. These terrible pack fights where they fall like wolves on the one that is down. There is very little snow left now except in the gullies and the sheltered valleys.

Sunday was a beautiful day of dry warmth in the hollows and fresh sea wind on the tops. I climbed to the top of the high ridge beside the harbour bar. I caught two spiders that were sunning themselves on a rock. Beside a running stream I came on the horns and skeleton of a caribou. They had been there for some time and the bones were bleached white. At the top of the cliffs the wind was strong, and a peregrine falcon was sparring against it.

Mill Island and Salisbury were dreaming in the distant haze, their outlines nebulous with mirage. There was ice in the inlet below, the colour of blue glass, and in the open water the ice-pans gleamed on the ruffled blue. On the way back I spent nearly half an hour trying to find a turnstone's nest, with the parents calling at me and begging me to go away. We had an enormous feed of eider ducks' eggs when I got back to the Post. They were very good but very rich and one quickly tires of them.

June 26th–July 2nd.

On Monday we started to make a board-walk round the house. We toiled at this, and at intervals plastered green paint on the window sashes and the eaves. A few mosquitoes appeared but did not do us any violence. One day was so warm that we worked naked to the waist. We suffered for it afterwards, as our backs were burnt the colour of lobsters. On Saturday it began to rain and blow. The glass fell like a stone and on Sunday morning it was blowing half a gale with rain.

Pitsulak came in with a boatload of Eskimos. The rougher the weather the more he likes it. He brought in some magnificent carvings—a walrus tusk faced off on either side with a picture of a dog team on it, and the figure of a woman as a companion to the carving that he did of myself. Putting the two carvings side by side I look puny and ineffective clutching a snow-knife, while my large strapping wife holds a long fish-spear and towers over me.

177

Pitsulak's companions looked an unhappy collection. They stood in their sodden sealskins looking like drowned rats, smiling faintly when one caught their eye. All Chesley's endeavours to persuade them not to come in on Sundays have been useless. In they come, more often than on any other day, and ruin our Sunday peace. They brought a few sealskins and some bundles of skin line to trade. They munched their biscuits in the back porch while their sodden clothes dripped. The ice is gone outside our harbour and here it is cracked and rotten but still strong enough to bear a dog team, and we are into July now.

July 3rd–9th.

This week we expected the flies, but, thank Heaven, they did not materialize! There are various reasons for that. The ice is still in the harbour and the wind that seldom leaves us alone has a chill edge to it. But the first warm day will bring them out in their myriads.

The ice is still in the harbour but has broken loose and floats in an enormous pan back and forth with the tides, unable to get out of the bottle neck. The wind pushes it ashore at high tide, and as the tide falls that part which comes to rest on the land splits off and breaks up. It lies there like pieces of a huge jig-saw puzzle until the next high tide carries it away.

We still do our regular promenade in the evenings, up the hill behind the Post until we look out on the strait. I collect a few plants for my press and we look at the ice. The big floating pan in the harbour has a curious pattern suggesting a backcloth on the stage showing a rough sea. The pools of water on the ice show grey-blue and the white of the ice runs in long white billowy patterns from one side to the other. A seal comes up occasionally and lies on the ice. Through the glasses you can watch the seal taking his rest. He lies on his side every now and then throwing up his head, his whole body rigid with attention, then down goes his head again. Uneasy sleeps a seal on the ice! The natives have killed two in the past week, while we watched them from the Post. As usual the dogs sat, ears pricked, tense and rigid watching the stalk. The women stood between the dogs and the ice driving them back with stones, every time they tried to rush. The figure doubled behind his white screen, crept forward, stopping every time the seal raised its head, making a yard or two when the seal lay down again. Then, when he was near enough, planting his screen and sitting down behind it with his elbows on his knees. Through the glasses I would watch the seal raise its head for the last time and then drop it. The hunter would be on his feet and running towards his quarry before the sound of the shot drifted back to us.

Otoochie shot one early one morning and wounded it. The shock of the bullet must have bemused it for it did not dive down its hole but into a shallow pool on the ice beside it. This was a curious mistake for an animal who acts only by instinct and who depends for life on the certainty of its reactions to alarm or danger.

Early one morning the Eskimos brought in a baby hare. It can only have been a week or two old. Chesley was cooking the breakfast and I was still in bed. I opened one eye to see Chesley standing over me with the little hare in his cupped hands. Two little dark eyes and two furry ears fronting a vague hump of soft grey-white fur. Chesley slipped him into my bed and he snuggled up beside me only too pleased to be warm and sheltered. After breakfast I took him back to where the natives found him. I carried him in my cupped hands while he looked about him. Sometimes he tried to bite, but his teeth were only like tiny blunt thorns. It was rather a pleasant sensation than otherwise. I put him down where the stony valley above Opalukta runs down to the sea. He sat quite motionless and then set off in a jerky gallop, a series of quick starts, like a clockwork rabbit. In a few seconds he was one with the grey rocks.

On Saturday the *Nascopie* left Montreal for the North. It gave me quite a pang to think of her coming to take me away. I have been very happy here.

Etidlooie killed a seal on the ice on Sunday morning when

the ice was pressed against the far shore, leaving a hundred yards of open water between its near side and the beach. Lugging the seal to the edge with his belt around its neck, he hauled it on to a floating ice-pan. Then, taking down his screen and using the wooden frame as a paddle, he set out for the shore. Fifteen yards away the wind turned against him and I had to go down and throw him a rope and haul him ashore.

We are tidying up the store for the ship's arrival. The loft seems light and empty, now that the furs are baled. In the winter there was a thick gloom in it. Snow was plastered on the window panes and from one end to the other ran the white foxes strung up in tens, 1,400 in all. There was a heap of over a hundred sealskins showing a tarnished silver. Ermine hung in a bunch, like ragged white plush. It was silent and cold and rather grim then. There were no eider ducks for Peter Scott.

July 10th–16th.

An Eskimo boat came in on Wednesday. They tied their boat up beside the ice in the harbour neck. They had practically nothing to trade, but stood about and smiled sheepishly. Old Pitolassie came in on Sunday for the second time in a week, weaving through the ice in his kayak. He brought me a wonderful collection of early Eskimo (Toonit) arrow heads.

We heard the *Nascopie* on the radio. She is approaching Port Burwell. It gives me a strange end-of-the-holiday feeling to hear her approaching. This place is becoming more glorious and beautiful day by day. Sunset turned the harbour to rippling gold and the bare rock of the mountains to a dusky purple. But I cannot stay long to admire it, as the flies drive one indoors.

13

THE LAST HUNT

July 17th–24th.

MONDAY was another day of perfect sunshine. In the evening we heard the chug of motor-boats. It was Pitsulak with the *Agpa* and Etoodluk with the *Keegarveealuk*. It was half tide. They came to within fifty yards of the shore and then threw their dogs into the water. We watched from the house. The dogs looked strange, ragged bundles disappearing in a cloud of glittering spray, to reappear as bobbing heads, pointed for the beach. There were scores and scores of dogs, and as each one shook himself he took his place among the spectators to watch the others. Pitsulak came up for a talk and we made our plans to leave on the next morning's tide.

Next morning saw us trundling petrol drums down to the water's edge, and loading sleeping-bags, food and rifles on board. And off we set. The tide was full and we crossed the bar without any trouble. There was quite a lot of ice on the other side, big scattered pans moving fast on the tide. We passed a big colony of kittiwakes nesting on the side of the cliffs. They were flying around in the cliff's shadow and their wings flashed white when they emerged into the sunlight. It was a day of bright sun, but the proximity of so much ice made it chilly.

Clear of the land we could see ice stretching out towards Salisbury Island. The water was deadly still out there, and every pan and hummock was reflected in it. We nosed our way down the water lanes, between the loose pans. Here and there were great patches of open water like still mill-ponds. Occasionally we saw the brown football head of a square-flipper, that big seal which runs up to 800 lbs. We had a man in the bows all the time on the look-out, sometimes two when we had to force off ice with poles and oars.

Twice we saw square-flippers on the ice. The first one dived
and I missed him. The second one was a monster. He kept on
dropping his head and lifting it to look round again. He had
heard our engines a long way off and had got used to it. I lay
on my face in the bows adjusting my sights as three hundred
yards changed to two hundred and then to one hundred.
Pitsulak sat, resting his elbows on his knees, ready to shoot.
At about a hundred yards distance the square-flipper gave us
a longer look than usual and prepared to dive. My bullet struck
him a split second before Pitsulak's. He made three plunges and
was in the water. He came up for air three times and each time
he managed to put an ice-pan between himself and the boat.
The fourth time he didn't and Pitsulak's bullet found his brain.
Square-flippers sink like stones at this season, but this one
caught and hung for perhaps five seconds on the submerged
spur of the pan beside which he had risen. We passed beside
him at full speed and Pitsulak let fly his harpoon. As we passed
we saw the square-flipper, a flabby shape on the pale ghostly
green of the spur. Pitsulak misjudged our speed. His harpoon
struck a foot to the side of the target, and the ivory head
shivered in pieces. We turned with all speed but the body had
slid away into the depths.

We boiled some tea and ate ship's biscuits for our luncheon.
The going got more and more difficult. The ice was changing.
It was no longer the small white pans of shore ice; big chunks
discoloured with mud were showing now. This was the heavy
ice from the Foxe Channel, which the whalers feared so much.
Our resistance to pressure was nil. Between two pieces of ice
we could be crushed like a match-box. We depended on
manoeuvring. We rigged up a chair with sealskin line and hauled
each other to the mast-head by turns. Five minutes was the
longest that one person could stand it, as the line began to cut
in to him after that. We would see a patch of open water and
steer for it, moving slowly through the ice, only to be met with
an impenetrable wall on the other side.

And so the afternoon slipped by. I had forgotten my watch

and we set Pitsulak's by the sun, making an error only of seven hours! Late afternoon saw us close to Mill Island, with Salisbury away to our left. The ice was heavy here, and ugly, and from the mast-head it seemed to stretch to the horizon. The sun cast a pale gold glow on the still water and gilded the distant ice. Occasionally a big piece would become top heavy and turn over, with a grinding thunder that turned to a hissing and petered away in a low muttering. We pushed eastward now until Salisbury Island lay on our other quarter. There was nothing doing here, absolutely nothing. Furthermore, we had brought only enough petrol to go straight to Nottingham and back, and this jockeying backwards and forwards had used up much already.

It was late when we supped off some tea and biscuit. It was damned cold, too. A chill came off the ice, a nasty damp chill. Pitsulak sat in the bows, rolling one cigarette after another, his dark eyes roving over the ice. Some seals bobbed up to look at us, and avoided a bullet just in time.

We drifted up against a large ice-pan and got out and stretched our legs. There was a pool of water on it and we filled our water-breaker. It was getting late, nearly midnight, or so we judged. Suddenly a seal, a very small one, bobbed up beside us. Pitsulak hit it in the back and we followed it. It came up to breathe just below where Pitsulak stood, harpoon in hand, like the figure of Nemesis. So close was he that he drove the harpoon clean through the seal, up to the wooden shaft. It looked small, and skinny, and pathetic as we hauled it out.

We all started to get sleepy. I asked Pitsulak if it would be safe to sleep now; his dark eyes twinkled as he shook his head. He brought his hands slowly together with an expressive gesture. "The ice", he said. I turned in, though, lay down in my clothes and pulled a deerskin and two sealskins over me. As I fell asleep I heard the puffing of the Primus stove. They were boiling up a feed of seal meat.

I awoke once to the cracking of rifle shots and the stamping of feet overhead and then I drifted off again. It was late morning

when I awoke again. The Eskimos had eaten most of the seal
and we were in the same position. During the night two square-
flippers had been killed, but they had both sunk like stones.
"It can't be helped," said Pitsulak, "We must go home." I went
back to sleep again. When I awoke again we were just off the
Cape and hardly moving against a full ebb-tide. There were big
scattered pans of ice racing along in the tide stream. We hung
against the current only moving perceptibly. It was hours
before we got into the Post.

Tookeke was in from Kungitijuak with his big boat and
a crowd of natives. Saila arrived the following day from
Nuwata. The ice had been bad and they had sprung a leak, "It
was no consequence", he said. Nothing is of any consequence
to the Eskimos. Munnome came in the evening by kayak.

We hauled up Tookeke's boat on Thursday afternoon. It
was a long job. Everybody hauled including the women, and
including poor old Pudlalik, Saila's brother, who is almost
blind and on crutches. He hobbled into position beside the rope
and put one old withered hand on it.

The mosquitoes bit us and an egregious old woman called
Mukshowjuk complicated matters by going down the line and
shaking hands with everybody. Later in the day she climbed up
a ladder that was against the big tanks. The children, who had
been waiting for this, rushed to the ladder and started to shake
it. The old woman's yells brought Chesley out, and he frightened
the children away.

Next evening the dogs ate a net. Chesley was so furious that
we very nearly had a row because he threatened to shoot the
dogs. He did not mean it, though. We heard on the radio that
the ship has changed her course and will not be here until
Thursday, but that Ralph Parsons, the Fur Trade Commissioner,
will be aboard.

On Sunday we went round the Eskimo tents. There was an
open-air service at which we nearly froze. One Eskimo after
another rose and testified. Occasionally we all rose to drone a
hymn, and all the time a chilly breeze was blowing. We went

round all the tents. Some were the old style skin "tents". I saw many friends. Old Amenuke was there. He was making a throwing-stick for me. A little boy came up to me without a thumb. He had cut it off with a snow-knife while cutting wood in the spring. I dressed it as best I could. Many faces were there that I had seen in winter snow houses. Two old women came in to see us. They knelt on the floor and crooned thanks for the mugs of tea we gave them. We gave them some biscuits each. They blessed us and crooned as they knelt. They told us all their troubles and all their jobs, what they were doing and were going to do. At last they got up and wrung our hands. "We are going to see our old friend Nee", they said. Nee is Saila's wife. A fine old woman of the primeval Eskimo type, tattooed face and hair flowing over her shoulders, a devout Christian and a fine chieftainess.

Josephie, the boy who hacked off his thumb, comes every day for me to treat him. He sits meekly holding out his shattered hand, like a dog with a sore paw, while I dress it. His eyes are sick with misery and he is beginning to acquire that look of patient suffering that gives so much nobility to the crippled Eskimo.

I went to the tents of Etidlooie and Otoochie to give them small presents; sun spectacles for Etidlooie, a handkerchief for his wife, and a hood for his small son. For Otoochie there was a tin box with a lock and key, a pocket-knife for his wife, and a body-belt for his young son. The men were out, so I gave the gifts to their wives and they thanked me with a politeness that would have done credit to the French.

185

14

THE ROAD HOME

A WEEK later the *Nascopie* arrived. The Eskimos who were watching from the cliffs of Opalukta pelted down to us, shouting, "The ship! The ship!" Chesley and I looked at each other in silence. A very happy partnership was almost at an end. Slowly and carefully we shaved and put on our better clothes.

Then nothing seemed to happen. We sat down to a game of cards, and talked with stilted formality. We had begun to forget about the ship, when suddenly a murmur of sound came from the assembly of Eskimos and husky dogs. She was gliding into the cove, looking black and gigantic beside the craft to which we were accustomed.

The surface frothed as she reversed her engines, and the echoes answered to the clanking as the anchor chains went down. We got into the dinghy with care. It took perhaps twenty turns to start the outboard motor. We made a long sweep past her and then back. She seemed to stand above us like a wall.

We climbed the companion way. At the top, Ralph Parsons, the Fur Trade Commissioner, shook our hands under the stare of alien eyes, and led us to his cabin.

I spilt my glass of sherry. For some reason my hand shook.

Then the familiar turmoil began. The winches began to clank as, with the slings out, next year's supplies were put over the side prior to taking on board our fur catch of the year that was past. There were many questions to answer. Several of the ship's company went ashore and examined carefully the house we had built.

It did not take long to unload the stores or to swing our catch on board. Then the *Nascopie* weighed anchor. Chesley stood at the top of the companion way. Behind and below him the sea swarmed with kayaks. It was as poignant a parting as ever I remember. His broad back in the red duffle dickie went down the companion. Then he was in the dinghy and the ladder was pulled up.

He was waving from the beach as the cove closed behind the wake of the ship, and hid him from sight.

From the kayaks there was a waving of hands and a chorus of good-byes that grew fainter and fainter. The granite cliffs of Opalukta passed in procession. Soon it was all fading into one strip of coastline etched in clear detail against the Northern Light.

I stood beside the rail until the coastline had sunk to a dim blue line along the horizon's edge. Somebody was trying to talk to me. It was about Munich.

I wasn't interested.

Six weeks later I was being measured for a uniform.